The
curious world of
CHRISTMAS

www.**rbooks**.co.uk

The
curious world of
CHRISTMAS

Celebrating all that is weird,
wonderful and festive

Niall Edworthy

Doubleday

LONDON • NEW YORK • TORONTO • SYDNEY • AUCKLAND

TRANSWORLD PUBLISHERS
61–63 Uxbridge Road, London W5 5SA
A Random House Group Company
www.rbooks.co.uk

First published in Great Britain
in 2007 by Doubleday
an imprint of Transworld Publishers

A CIP catalogue record for this book
is available from the British Library.

ISBN 9780385612692

Addresses for Random House Group Ltd companies outside the UK
can be found at: www.randomhouse.co.uk
The Random House Group Ltd Reg. No. 954009

The Random House Group Ltd makes every effort to ensure that the papers used in
its books are made from trees that have been legally sourced from well-managed and
credibly certified forests. Our paper procurement policy can be found at:
www.randomhouse.co.uk/paper.htm

Set in 10/12pt Mrs Eaves Roman by
Falcon Oast Graphic Art Ltd

Printed in Great Britain by Clays Ltd, Bungay, Suffolk
Design layouts by Fiona Andreanelli (www.andreanelli.com)

2 4 6 8 10 9 7 5 3 1

Mixed Sources
Product group from well-managed
forests and other controlled sources
www.fsc.org Cert no. TT-COC-2139
© 1996 Forest Stewardship Council
FSC

For Alfie and Eliza

Thanks

It is impossible to put together a book of this nature without a great deal of help from a great many people. My first thanks must go to Susanna Wadeson, my editor, who came up with the idea for the book and, as ever, was so imaginative and helpful in her original suggestions and feedback. Thanks too to the production and sales teams at Transworld, especially Deborah Adams, Manpreet Grewal, Fiona Andreanelli, Sheila Lee and Geraldine Ellison, and to Lucy Davie who produced the lovely design for the cover. I owe a further debt of gratitude to the unsung archivists at the Imperial War Museum and their equally helpful cousins at the British Library in St Pancras and the newspaper library in Colindale, London. Thanks once again (for the eighteenth time now!) to my agent, Araminta Whitley at Lucas Alexander Whitley. Long may her advice continue to be even more sensible than her shoes.

Contents

Love It or Loathe It:

Introduction

IT IS A GREAT PARADOX OF CHRISTMAS THAT IT SHOULD PROMISE US all a period of tremendous harmony, peace and fun, and yet, to a minority in our midst, it somehow manages to deliver nothing but anxiety and ill-feeling. For the Christmas grumblers, the annual winter holiday is not a generous gift in life's stocking, it's a lump of coal; a holiday period so intolerable that a return to the drudgery and routine of the workplace in the dark days of January never comes soon enough. These curmudgeons are the direct descendants of the dramatist George Bernard Shaw, whose feverish denunciations of the festive season always came speckled with a shower of froth: *I am sorry to have to introduce the subject of Christmas*, the Irishman spat. *It is an indecent subject; a cruel, gluttonous subject; a wicked, cadging, lying, filthy, blasphemous, and demoralizing subject.*

With his long white beard and dancing eyes he may well have looked like Santa's skinny younger brother, but no one in history has despised Christmas quite as intensely as Shaw. Not even the seventeenth-century Puritans, who went so far as to ban its celebration for 15 years. Nor the billions of non-Christians, who choose to ignore it, tolerate it and look upon it from a distance with a mildly bemused indifference. (The Japanese, bless them, even join in the celebrations.) Not even Vexen Crabtree, Britain's most high-profile Satanist, loathes Christmas like Shaw loathed it. Vexen feels only indifference towards the celebration of Christ's nativity and reportedly still eats his turkey dinner on the day.

As a socialist, Shaw was riled by the materialism and consumerism of the holiday period and what he saw as an all-too-brief flash of middle-class charity towards the poor and less fortunate; as an atheist turned mystic, he must have been repelled by the overtly Christian dimension of the holiday; as a radical rationalist, he will no doubt have been appalled by its superstitious pagan elements and the absurdity of Father Christmas and his airborne reindeer. As a serious dramatist and man of letters, he was horrified by the immense silliness of the Christmas pantomime – and all the other quaint, unintellectual, sentimental and indulgent aspects that the season brings us by the sleigh-load. As a devout vegetarian and teetotaller, perhaps it was his physical disgust at the thought of all that roasted animal flesh and booze that excited his bile.

No one has articulated their scorn for Christmas quite as powerfully or wittily as Shaw, but there has always been a very vocal minority who share at least some of his views on the subject and no doubt there always will be. In a strange way, the Christmas moaners have become as much a feature of the season as a turkey lunch or a well-decorated tree. Somehow it wouldn't be quite the same without them.

There is of course another type of Christmas extremist, an altogether happier chap for whom the annual winter holiday is a perfectly smashing, absolutely wizard occasion. He is the Christmas fanatic who will beat you over the head with turkey drumsticks until he pops out of his Santa suit if you so much as whisper a word of of weariness about the world's largest religious festival. He is simply nutty for Noël. (I say 'he'

advisedly because these 'crazy' Christmas cavorters are rarely female.) You can spot a Noël Nutter from 100 paces. He will be the one at the Christmas party wearing some combination of the following: a) a jumper or tie with a pattern of reindeers mating; b) comedy glasses which squirt snow and then wipe the lenses with built-in wipers; and c) a revolving bow tie.

In all likelihood, the Noël Nutter's front garden — and probably his roof — will be crammed with every imaginable item of Christmas kitsch: an eight-foot-high light-up inflatable snowman, a Santa sleigh with full set of reindeer and *faux* presents, several thousand outdoor lights and a road sign reading Santa Stop Here! *Christmas Prat*, I think, is the proper scientific term for this species and I'm not sure I'd invite him round for a Christmas drink any sooner than I would the whingers in the Shaw camp. To some extent, the Christmas Prat is the very reason why the Shavian moaners come over all gloomy and break out in a rash each December. Remove the Prat — and all who encourage and sell to him — and you remove a great deal of the reason to dislike Christmas.

Somewhere in between these two groups of extremists who have unwittingly joined forces and done their best to despoil the image of

our ancient winter festival, you will find the rest of us: a vast global population of people living in predominantly Christian cultures for whom Christmas remains, by and large, and if celebrated properly, a truly joyful period of the year.

On a superficial level, Christmas is a time when the ordinary rules of daily life are suspended for a week or two, when the tools of work are laid down and the workplace vacated, when scattered families and old friends gravitate to each other's

homes to exchange gifts and greetings, when miserable diets and boring exercise programmes are abandoned and we can eat and drink ourselves daft, when strangers treat each other with greater kindness and civility, when fireplaces, candles and decorations bring some warmth and cheer against the cold and bleak landscape outside, when a sense of brotherhood and kindness towards the less fortunate is roused, when television and theatre try even harder to entertain us, when fair-weather and lapsed Christians can enjoy going to church without feeling a little uncertain as to whether or not they should be there ... For the truly devout among us, the Christmas period is of course a wonderful and highly significant time in the calendar, even without any of the above. Falling where it does, the Christmas holiday period also has the virtue of drawing a line under one year and stirring up promise and hope for another, wiping clean the slate of our experience, and allowing us to start all over again and have another bash at getting our lives right. Christmas also acts as a milestone, or a marker, in our family lives, tracking our development and relationships over the years.

These are all great reasons to look forward to Christmas and to cherish every day of it when it comes, and when the often stressful business of preparing, organizing and staging it allows. But it seems there is something far deeper at work in this anticipation and enjoyment, something more than plain physical indulgence and holiday-time recreation. What is it about the sound of a distant carol floating on the air, the smell of a freshly carved turkey or a pan of mulled wine, or the sight of a snow-bound landscape or a tastefully decorated pine tree that excites, for so many of us, such feelings of warmth, reassurance and expectation? The answer, I think, is found in the past: the past of our own lives *and* in the wider, deeper past of our civilization, our history, our roots.

On the face of it, 25 December is a date in a religious calendar when Christians celebrate the birth of Christ, a central day of religious observation that has expanded into a longer, more secularized holiday period. The truth, however, is far more complicated and interesting. Most of us are dimly aware that there are elements of pagan ritual blended into the Christian and commercialized secular customs of the holiday. It is well known, for instance, that the practice of hanging up mistletoe in our homes has some connection with the Druids. What I hadn't understood before setting out to research this collection was quite *how many* of our Christmas traditions are pagan in origin, stretching back thousands of years, deep into the past of European civilization. These ancient customs, many of them linked to winter solstice festivals, were

absorbed into the Christian experience. Over the centuries they have been modified, moulded and repackaged to the point where we now think of them as being mainly Christian in origin, with just a hint of paganism about them.

In truth, it's the other way round. There is no criticism of the Church, or disappointment, in this observation. On the contrary, I find it exciting that whenever we bring a Christmas tree or some holly branches into our homes, when we exchange gifts with one another, when we light our candles and fires, when we throw a Christmas party or lay on a feast, we are performing a modern-day version of our distant ancestors' winter celebrations. I may not wear an animal-skin loincloth or live in a wattle-and-daub hut or hunt and gather my own food — well, not since my university days at any rate — but the way I celebrate Christmas links me, through

dozens of centuries, with
my primeval forebears.
Over the centuries, various
cultures and civilizations
have contributed to the
constantly changing
nature of Christmas:
Romans, Persians, Celts,
Norsemen, medieval kings
and noblemen, Puritans
and Parliamentarians,
enterprising Victorians,
German princes, American
settlers, to name but some.
I cannot think of any other
event that manages to
connect us to our earliest

roots as directly as all the rituals of Christmas.

Above all else, though, Christmas is about children and it is
this association with innocence, the link with our own childhood,
that is the most evocative and emotive aspect of the season. Our
prime concern as adults is that the children, especially the younger
ones, have a memorable and happy time. It's difficult not to share
their sense of mounting excitement as the year advances and first
the Christmas period and then the day itself approaches. (By the
same token, it's easy to understand why people without children
rarely show great enthusiasm for Christmas; I wonder whether it's
significant that Bernard Shaw never produced a family.) By entering
into the spirit of Christmas, we allow ourselves to indulge briefly in
a world of innocence and in a childlike sense of wonder. That purity
of feeling was stolen from us when we became world-weary grown-
ups, but at Christmas we can suspend our scepticism and cynicism,
forget the harsher world of adult experience for a while, surrender
ourselves to sentimentality and join in the awe and the wonder and
the excitement. In short, we become children again. There's nothing
cool or clever about liking Christmas, and that, I suspect, is what
I like about it. I'm with Charles Dickens, not Bernard Shaw, on
this one: *Christmas time! That man must be a misanthrope indeed in whose breast
something like a jovial feeling is not roused — in whose mind some pleasant associations
are not awakened — by the recurrence of Christmas.*

Farting Dwarves and Peacock Pie:

How Our Ancestors Celebrated Christmas

THE DATE OF CHRIST'S BIRTH HAS BEEN a matter of dispute for centuries, but most scholars agree that 25 December is a suspiciously convenient point in the calendar. The date just happens to be the day of the winter solstice in the old Julian calendar, when pagans across Europe and the Middle East celebrated the birth of the new sun with a series of ceremonies, feasts and wild parties. It also marked the end of

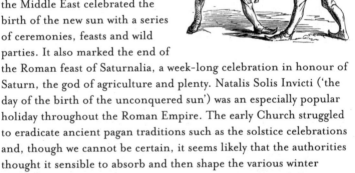

the Roman feast of Saturnalia, a week-long celebration in honour of Saturn, the god of agriculture and plenty. Natalis Solis Invicti ('the day of the birth of the unconquered sun') was an especially popular holiday throughout the Roman Empire. The early Church struggled to eradicate ancient pagan traditions such as the solstice celebrations and, though we cannot be certain, it seems likely that the authorities thought it sensible to absorb and then shape the various winter festivals into a Christian form, rather than alienate people by banishing them altogether.

❄ ❄ ❄ ❄

THE ROMAN HOLIDAY OF **SATURNALIA** HAD DEVELOPED INTO A WILD festival starting on 17 December and ending with the winter solstice celebrations, during which time only cooks and bakers were allowed to work. Even slaves were freed from their duties to join in the revelry, which included street processions, fire and torch ceremonies, lavish feasts, dressing up in animal skins and other costumes and a great deal of drinking. There followed a few days' break to recuperate before the Romans launched themselves into the **Kalends** celebrations, the equivalent of our New Year, which rivalled Saturnalia for revelry and drunkenness. During the end-of-year holiday the Romans also exchanged gifts and decorated their homes with evergreens, just as we do at Christmas today.

Handily, many of the Roman traditions of Saturnalia lent themselves to Christian interpretation. The holly with which people bedecked their homes came to represent Christ's crown of thorns, and the giving of presents was a symbol of Jesus Christ as God's gift to man. Even the pagan tradition of scattering corn and straw throughout the home was easily Christianized because it reminded worshippers of Christ's lowly surroundings in the Bethlehem stable.

❄ ❄ ❄ ❄

NOWHERE IN THE GOSPELS OR THE WRITINGS of the early Christians is there any mention of Christ's birthday. It was several centuries after his lifetime that the date became a matter of conjecture and argument. This was partly because **early Christians had no interest in birthdays.** The Epiphany (today, 6 January) was of greater importance: in the Eastern Churches, this was the day for celebrating Christ's baptism; in the West it was to commemorate the manifestation of Christ's glory and his revelation to the Magi. Some early Christians even took exception to the recognition of birthdays because it distracted from their more significant 'deathdays', when saints were martyred and Christ had given his life for mankind. Exactly when the Church decided upon 25 December as the birth date of Jesus is unclear, but it almost certainly came to be accepted as that during the fourth century, possibly during the reign of Constantine, the first Christian Roman emperor.

*The ancient peoples of the Angli began the year
on the 25th of December when we now celebrate
the birthday of the Lord; and the very night which
is now so holy to us, they called in their tongue,
'modranecht', that is, the mother's night, by reason
we suspect of the ceremonies which in that night-
long vigil they performed.*

ST BEDE (c. 673-735)
De Temporum Ratione

❄ ❄ ❄ ❄

*The outgoing of the Romans and the incoming of the Angles, the Saxons and
the Jutes, disastrously affected the festival of Christmas, for the invaders were
heathens, and Christianity was swept westward before them. They lived in a part
of the Continent which had not been reached by Christianity nor classic culture
and they worshipped the false gods of Woden and Thunder and were addicted
to various heathenish practices, some of which are mingled with the festivities of
Christmastide ... The Anglo-Saxon excesses are referred to by some of the old
chroniclers, intemperance being a very prevalent vice at the Christmas festival.
Ale and mead were their favourite drinks; wines were used as occasional luxuries.*

W. F. DAWSON
Christmas: Its Origins and Associations, **1902**

❄ ❄ ❄ ❄

IN THE MIDDLE AGES, THE CHURCH JOINED IN THE GENERAL REVELRY
at Christmas time with some very peculiar and irreligious traditions
of its own. One such was the custom of the **Boy Bishop**. At the
beginning of December, usually 6 December (St Nicholas's Day),
in cathedrals across Britain and Europe, a young choirboy was
elected to be bishop until the 28th, Holy Innocents' Day. He was
chosen either by the bishop or by his fellow choristers, depending
on the cathedral, and for three weeks the young boy, dressed in
cope and mitre and carrying a crook, travelled the diocese with his
high-pitched soprano chums, carrying out a number of grown-up
duties. The election of the boy drew huge crowds to the cathedral
and there was much hilarity as the senior clergy swapped places
with the choristers. After the service, there followed a lavish feast
at which the choristers were allowed to eat as much food and drink

as much wine as they wished. This was the high point of the year for medieval choristers, who led a harsh, thankless life otherwise. Their days were usually long and hard, they were often fed poorly and they were frequently beaten by their masters. During his travels, the Boy Bishop visited monasteries and larger churches, preaching sermons written for him by a senior clergyman. The tradition of the Boy Bishop was disliked by many within the Church, but others justified it on the grounds that it demonstrated vividly how the lowly and meek were able to acquire authority and respect, just as Jesus had done in his life. The Boy Bishop tradition was ended in Britain during the reign of Queen Elizabeth I, but continued for almost another 200 years elsewhere in Europe.

❄ ❄ ❄ ❄

THE MEAT OF THE **PEACOCK** IS TOUGH, DRY AND UNAPPETIZING BUT that didn't seem to bother the royals and nobles of the Middle Ages. To them, the Indian forest bird was a spectacular speciality, and it was served up in the dining halls of castles and baronial homes amid great pomp and ceremony. Often the bird was made into a large pie with the head sticking out through the crust at one end and its huge feathery tail sticking out of the other. Cooks sometimes discarded the meat of the peacock altogether and filled the pies with tastier birds such as goose and chicken.

❄ ❄ ❄ ❄

CHRISTMAS DAY 1066: 'THE BASTARD' BECAME 'THE CONQUEROR' when William I was crowned King of England at Westminster Abbey. When the Norman contingent at the ceremony was asked by Ealdred, the Archbishop of York, if they welcomed William as king, the shouts of approval were so loud that the guards outside suspected treachery of some kind and immediately set about torching nearby buildings. Historian Orderic Vitalis records that the fire spread so fast that most of the congregation fled: *Only the bishops and a few clergy and monks remained, terrified in the sanctuary, and with difficulty completed the*

consecration of the king who was trembling from head to foot. William's funeral in Caen Abbey 21 years later was no less dramatic. William's corpse, too fat for his coffin, burst midway through the service, filling the abbey with 'an unbearable stench', according to Vitalis.

CAROL SINGERS were generally shunned by medieval clergy and barred from most churches on the grounds that the practice was more pagan than Christian. The carollers, who danced in a circle as they sang, were forced to pursue their revelry out in the streets, moving from house to house.

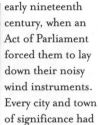

❋ ❋ ❋ ❋

28 DECEMBER IS 'HOLY Innocents' Day' or 'Childermass Day', when the Church commemorates the children allegedly killed on the order of King Herod. It has been regarded as a day of ill omen from the Middle Ages onwards. Edward IV postponed his coronation to another day and Louis XI of France refused to conduct business on it, while superstitious people claim that no one should be married or start building a house on the dreaded day. Some records suggest that young English boys were beaten on Holy Innocents' Day to remind them of Herod's savagery.

❋ ❋ ❋ ❋

'WAITS' (TOWN PIPERS) were a common sight and sound from medieval times until the early nineteenth century, when an Act of Parliament forced them to lay down their noisy wind instruments. Every city and town of significance had a **band of waits** and their duties included heralding the arrival of royal guests at the town gates, or leading the mayor's parades. Their habit of wandering the streets in the dead of night and striking up a windy tune under people's windows wasn't universally appreciated, and there were few protests when the Municipal Corporations Act of 1835 forced their abolition. Like a bad smell, however, the waits lingered in the air a while longer, turning up at Christmas time to sing and play carols for money until the early twentieth century.

❋ ❋ ❋ ❋

The only music I have heard this week is waits; to sit up working until two or three in the morning, and then — just as I am losing myself in my first sleep — to hear 'Venite Adoremus' welling forth from a cornet English pitch, a saxhorn Society of Arts pitch (or thereabouts), and a trombone French pitch, is the sort of thing that breaks my peace and destroys my goodwill towards men!

Diaries of GEORGE BERNARD SHAW (1856-1950), Irish dramatist and essayist

THE EXPRESSION 'HUMBLE PIE' originates from a medieval Christmas practice whereby the rich gave the innards of their deer to the poor as a treat. The offal was known as the 'umbles', and the grateful peasants used it to make a pie. Christmas Day was not all unfettered joy in the hovels of the poor, as it happened to be one of the calendar's four 'quarter days' when tenants were obliged to pay his lordship his rent and taxes.

✼ ✼ ✼ ✼

DURING THE MIDDLE AGES, THE tables of the rich would have been filled with a sumptuous display of foods throughout the 12 days of Christmas. **Goose** was a common dish and the bird was often given a shiny, golden appearance by basting it in a mixture of butter and the highly coveted and expensive spice, saffron. **Pork or wild boar** often formed the *pièce de résistance* of the Christmas feast, and the roasts were carried into the dining halls amid great fanfare with lemons stuffed into the beasts' mouths.

✼ ✼ ✼ ✼

THE MURDER IN 1170 OF THE Archbishop of Canterbury, **Thomas à Becket,** as he prayed in his cathedral was considered all the more horrendous for its having occurred during the Christmas period. Taking King Henry II's plea – 'Will no one rid me of this turbulent priest?' – to its logical conclusion, four knights of his court rode straight to Canterbury on 29 December and murdered Becket in the cathedral's north transept.

✼ ✼ ✼ ✼

IF YOUR CHILDREN MOAN AS YOU drag them away from their toys and off to church on Christmas Day, remind them of the experiences suffered by their youthful ancestors in the Middle Ages. 'Christ's Mass', the celebration of the Nativity established in the seventh century, consisted of **three services**: one at midnight (the Angel's Mass), one at dawn (the Shepherd's Mass), and the third at some point during the day (the Mass of the Divine Word).

FROM WILLIAM THE CONQUEROR THROUGH TO THE EARLY SEVENTEENTH century, the feast of the Epiphany, on 6 January, was celebrated far more lavishly than Christmas Day owing to its associations with the notion of kingship. It is the day that the Church celebrated the showing of Christ 'the King' to the Three Kings, Caspar, Melchior and Balthasar. For centuries and until modern times, in many countries, including Britain, it was customary to **exchange gifts on the Epiphany**, not on the Nativity.

❋ ❋ ❋ ❋

IN THE LATE TWELFTH CENTURY, HENRY II HAD A FOOL CALLED Roland le Pettour (Roland the Farter), whose antics he enjoyed so much that he used to force him out of retirement on Christmas Day to perform his *saltum, siffletum et pettum* routine (a leap, a whistle and a fart). Two centuries on, William Langland wrote in *Piers Plowman* of minstrels **farting in harmony** with their pipes to amuse their noble patrons during the Christmas festivities.

❋ ❋ ❋ ❋

THE ROYAL CHRISTMAS FEAST OF 1214 IS A SIGNIFICANT MOMENT IN British history, for it was then that England's barons laid down their demands to King John for what became the Magna Carta.

Janus sits by the fire with double beard,
And drinketh of his bugle horn the wine:
Before him stands the brawn of tusk-ed swine.
And 'Nowel' cryeth every lusty man.

Chaucer's only reference to Christmas, in 'The Franklin's Tale'
Canterbury Tales

❋ ❋ ❋ ❋

When Richard II entertained King Leon of Armenia at the Royal Palace, Eltham, over Christmas 1386, he laid on a **feast** of great extravagance, feeding 10,000 guests over 12 days with 28 oxen, 300 sheep and thousands of game birds and fowl.

❋ ❋ ❋ ❋

During his siege of Rouen in 1418, Henry V suspended operations on Christmas Day and delivered food for the hungry inhabitants.

❋ ❋ ❋ ❋

Until the nineteenth century people used to keep up their **holly and ivy**, and other evergreen decorations, until Candlemas on 2 February, which officially marks the end of the Christmas period according to the Christian calendar. Candlemas commemorates the ritual purification of Mary, 40 days after Christ's birth, and evolved from an ancient Jewish belief that women were unclean after the birth of a child. Women weren't allowed to worship in the temple for 40 days after giving birth to a boy and for 60 days if it was a girl, after which they had to be cleansed. It is known as Candlemas because it was on this day that all the church's candles for the year were blessed, and many homes placed candles on their windowsills. Like many Christmas traditions, Candlemas was a bastardized Christian version of a pagan tradition. For centuries, millennia even, pagans had celebrated the festival of light at this time of year as it marked the halfway point of winter, between the winter solstice and the spring equinox.

FROM THE MIDDLE AGES TO THE Tudor period, the English monarch traditionally invited dozens of the nobility to join the royal court in lavish and lengthy celebrations over the Christmas period. Great offence was given by those who declined the invitation, and the only acceptable excuses were war, childbirth and life-threatening illness. Queen Elizabeth I was especially insistent that her male courtiers left their wives at home and joined her for the full 12 days of festivities. A royal banquet could feature as many as 20 courses, and kitchens were obliged to cook far more than the guests could eat so that a generous surplus might be distributed to the poor when their lordships could eat or drink no more, and had moved on to tossing the court dwarves and throwing scraps to the minstrels. Often, the local townsfolk were allowed into the dining hall to put on a sort of **variety performance** for the King or Queen, featuring jugglers, magicians, mummers (mimers), musicians and bards.

❄ ❄ ❄ ❄

THE FEAST OF FOOLS, LIKE THE TRADITION OF THE BOY BISHOP, was a bizarre medieval Christmas practice that can have done little to promote the dignity of the clergy. In an ecclesiastical version of an office party crossed with a pantomime, members of the lower clergy (usually peasants) dressed up as animals, women, bishops, and sometimes even the Pope, and set about mocking their higher-ranking colleagues and the Church's most sacred institutions. There was much **licence and buffoonery** throughout the pageant, which usually took place on or about the Feast of the Circumcision (1 January). More often known by its Latin name, Festum Fatuorum, the festival, which was especially popular in France, was considered blasphemous by the more serious-minded within the Church. The pagan roots of the tradition, with their echoes of the raucous Roman

Saturnalia, were a further cause of disquiet and the comic custom was finally forbidden, under pain of the harshest penalties, by the Council of Basle in 1435.

❄ ❄ ❄ ❄

THE MEDIEVAL CHRISTMAS TRADITION OF **'wassailing'** has all but died out in England. The word derives from the Old English words *wæs* and *hæl*, meaning 'be healthy' or 'be whole' (as in 'hale and hearty'). Originally, a wassail ceremony, or toast, celebrated the new rising of the sun following the winter solstice, and encouraged a bountiful harvest of fruit in the coming year. By Tudor times, wassailing often took the form of bands of half-cut peasants staggering between the houses of richer folk, singing carols and refusing to leave until they had been rewarded for their efforts with a gift or a donation of hard cash. The wassailers' demand for figgy pudding in the traditional English song 'We Wish You A Merry Christmas' is followed by the menacing 'We won't go until we get some!'

❄ ❄ ❄ ❄

THE TRADITIONAL 'WASSAIL' DRINK ENJOYED BY OUR FOREBEARS comprised a mixture of **mulled ale, spices and the pulp of roasted apples** – and, it seems, anything else that was lying around, including curdled cream and eggs. The frothiness of the concoction explains its alternative name of 'lamb's wool'. There are still odd pockets of die-hard wassailers to be found in the West Country, defiantly singing and dancing beneath apple trees, performing curious quasi-pagan rituals and drinking to the health of apple trees in the hope that they may produce a better cider crop. The custom often takes place on the old Twelfth Night, 17 January.

❄ ❄ ❄ ❄

Let every man take off his hat
And shout out to th'old apple tree
'Old apple tree we wassail thee
And hoping thou will bear.'

WASSAILING SONG

LIKE SO MANY MEDIEVAL CHRISTMAS TRADITIONS, WASSAILING WAS suppressed during the Puritan crackdown on fun in the seventeenth century. In 1644, Oliver Cromwell's administration carried an Act of Parliament banning any form of celebration during the Twelve Days of Christmas, on the grounds that there is no mention of Christmas in the Bible. But it was the pagan elements and 'Popish' associations to which the Puritans took the most violent exception. The more extreme Puritans dubbed 25 December 'Satan's working day' and the 'Antichrist's Mass'. They even **banned mince pies** and the traditional evergreen decorations such as holly and ivy, and 'lust-inducing' mistletoe. Christmas officially became a gloomy day of work and fasting until 1660, when, to the great relief of the drinking classes, the monarchy was restored and Charles II sat on the throne. But Christmas was never quite the same again and it wasn't until the combined efforts of Prince Albert, Charles Dickens and a handful of Americans in the nineteenth century that the festive season rediscovered its medieval sense of joy.

❄ ❄ ❄

THE PURITAN WRITER WILLIAM PRYNNE HAD THIS TO SAY ABOUT Christmas festivities in 1633: *When our Saviour was borne into the world at first we hear of no feasting, drinking, healthing, carding, dicing, stage plays, mummeries, masques or heathenish Christmas pastimes; those puritanical angels, saints and shepherds knew no such pompous Christmas courtships which the devil and his accursed instruments have since appropriated to his most blessed Nativity.*

❄ ❄ ❄

THE DIARIST JOHN EVELYN, A PROTESTANT BUT NO PURITAN, WROTE this well-known account of his experiences when he went to observe the Nativity in a chapel off the Strand in 1657:

I went to London with my wife to celebrate Christmas Day. Sermon ended, the chapel was surrounded with soldiers. As we went up to receive the Sacrament, the miscreants held their muskets against us, as if they would have shot us at the altar: but yet suffering us to finish the office of Communion, as perhaps not having instructions what to do in case they found us in that action.

Evelyn was held for 24 hours for celebrating Christmas Day and reprimanded for his folly.

THE CALVINIST SCOTS OF THE sixteenth century were particularly severe in their denunciation of Christmas celebrations. Dourness had become a virtue north of the Tweed and never more so than when their frivolous, effete neighbours over the border were shaming themselves during December in wild, drunken revelry, lust and gluttony. Nearly a century before the Puritans took power in England after the Civil War, **the Scots had stamped out any semblance of Christmas fun** in their own land. Not that Christmas in Scotland had been a barrel of laughs beforehand. In 1575 magistrates in Aberdeen punished a group of girls for 'playing, dancing and singing of filthy carols on Yule Day'. It wasn't until 1958 that Christmas became a national holiday in Scotland.

✳ ✳ ✳ ✳

Perhaps no single circumstance more strongly illustrates the temper of the Precisians [Puritans] *than their conduct respecting Christmas Day. Christmas had been, from time immemorial, the season of joy and domestic affection, the season when families assembled, when children came home from school, when quarrels were made up, when carols were heard in every street, when every house was decorated with evergreens, and every table was loaded with good cheer. At that season all hearts not utterly destitute of kindness were enlarged and softened. At that season the poor were admitted to partake largely of the overflowings of the wealth of the rich, whose bounty was peculiarly acceptable on account of the shortness of the days and of the severity of the weather. At that season, the interval between landlord and tenant, master and servant, was less marked than through the rest of the year. Where there is much enjoyment there will be some excess: yet, on the whole, the spirit in which the holiday was kept was not unworthy of a Christian festival … No public act of that time seems to have irritated the common people more* [than the suppression of Christmas]. *On the next anniversary of the festival formidable riots broke out in many places. The constables were resisted, the magistrates insulted, the houses of noted zealots attacked, and the prescribed service of the day openly read in the churches.*

THOMAS BABINGTON MACAULAY
(1800–59)
The History of England from James II

THE PILGRIMS WHO CAME TO AMERICA IN THE EARLY 1600S WERE English Puritans, and even more zealous in their beliefs than those they left behind. Christmas was not a holiday for most early settlers and from 1659 to 1681 the celebration of it was banned by the courts in Boston. When the ban was lifted, those who took to celebrating the day were regarded with contempt. In 1687, the well-known Puritan Reverend Increase Mather wrote: *The generality of Christmas-keepers observe that festival after such a manner as is highly dishonourable to the name of Christ. How few are there comparatively that spend those holidays (as they are called) after an holy manner. But they are consumed in Compotations, in Interludes, in playing at Cards, in Revellings, in excess of Wine, in mad Mirth ...* As in England, Christmas never recovered its former glory after the Puritan purge. A century later, the House of Congress was in session on 25 December 1789, the first Christmas under America's new constitution, and it wasn't until 1870 that it was declared a federal holiday.

FROM 1558, ENGLISH CATHOLICS WERE PROHIBITED BY LAW TO practise their faith for almost three centuries and it wasn't until 1829, when an Act of Parliament sealed a growing cultural tolerance, that the emancipation of the 'Papists' was completed. Though some historians dispute the claim, others assert that 'The Twelve Days of Christmas' was a song written as a **coded memory aid** to help young Catholics learn the basics of their faith. According to the theory:

The partridge in the pear tree is the Son of God

Two turtle doves are the Old and New Testament

Three French hens, faith, hope and charity

Four calling birds, the four Gospels

Five golden rings, the first five books of the Old Testament (Pentateuch) chronicling Man's fall from grace

Six geese a'laying, the six days of creation

Seven swans a'swimming, seven gifts of the Holy Spirit and the seven sacraments

Eight maids a'milking, the eight Beatitudes from the Sermon on the Mount ('Blessed are the meek' etc.)

Nine ladies dancing, nine fruits of the Holy Spirit

Ten lords a'leaping, Ten Commandments

Eleven pipers piping, eleven faithful apostles

Twelve drummers drumming, twelve points of doctrine in the Apostles' Creed.

The diary of Samuel Pepys gives an insight into a middle-class Christmas in London, the year following the end of Puritan rule:

Wednesday 25 December 1661. In the morning to church, where at the door of our pew I was fain to stay, because that the sexton had not opened the door. A good sermon of Mr. Mills. Dined at home all alone, and taking occasion from some fault in the meat to complain of my maid's sluttery, my wife and I fell out, and I up to my chamber in a discontent. After dinner my wife comes up to me and all friends again, and she and I to walk upon the leads, and there Sir W. Pen called us, and we went to his house and supped with him, but before supper Captain Cock came to us half drunk, and began to talk, but Sir W. Pen knowing his humour and that there was no end of his talking, drinks four great glasses of wine to him, one after another, healths to the king, and by that means made him drunk, and so he went away, and so we sat down to supper, and were merry, and so after supper home and to bed.

From the end of Puritan domination in the late seventeenth century through to the early years of Queen Victoria's reign, Christmas Day for most people occasioned **far more subdued** celebrations than New Year's Day and Twelfth Night. To many, it was a day just like any other. The *Times* newspaper made no mention of the day between 1790 and 1835. The Christmas period had an obvious structure at this time, beginning with the holy day of the Nativity and ending with a wilder, more indulgent festival to celebrate Twelfth Night, on the eve of the Epiphany. Right in the middle of the period, there was an entirely non-religious day of drinking and dancing to see in the New Year.

Christmas goes out in fine style with Twelfth Night. It is a finish worthy of the time. Christmas Day was the morning of the season; New Year's Day the middle of it, or noon; Twelfth Night is the night, brilliant with innumerable planets of Twelfth-cakes. The whole island keeps court; nay, all Christendom. All the world are kings and queens. Everybody is somebody else, and learns at once to laugh at, and to tolerate, characters different from his own, by enacting them. Cakes, characters, forfeits, lights, theatres, merry rooms, little holiday-faces, and, last not least, the painted sugar on the cakes, so bad to eat but so fine to look at, useful because it is perfectly useless except for a sight and a moral — all conspire to throw a giddy splendour over the last night of the season, and to send it to bed in pomp and colours, like a Prince.

Leigh Hunt (1784–1859), on the Twelfth Cake

EACH REGION OF BRITAIN USED TO KEEP ITS
own peculiar Christmas customs over the years,
many of them variations upon a similar theme.
One such was the 'hodening' ceremony performed
in East Kent, most notably at Ramsgate, which
dates back to the end of the seventeenth century.
In its original form, hodening involved a group
of youngsters **fixing the head of a dead horse to
a pole**, attaching a piece of string to its lower jaw
and cloaking the pole in sackcloth to give it the
appearance of a very crude pantomime horse. One
of the group would then climb under and ride
the 'horse' around town, snapping its jaws open
and shut with the string while his chums, dressed
in grotesque costumes, ran alongside ringing hand-bells, shouting
and singing songs. Folklore historians are unsure of the significance
of this tradition. A similar Christmas ritual, known as Mari Lwyd
(Grey Mare), used to be performed at Christmas time throughout
rural Wales.

HIS FIRST PANTOMIME

Enthralled by his first pantomime
he thought his little world was crammed
tight with pleasure that night. But he
was wrong. Before mother gave him his
good-night kiss, she gave him his first
Kia-Ora (in hot water for the night was
cold). As he drained the glass to the
last delicious drop, his happiness was
really complete. It was the perfect end
to a perfect day. Mother! It's delicious!
Always ask your grocer for a bottle.

* * * *

*In South Cardiganshire it seems that about eighty
years ago the population, rich and poor, male and
female, of opposing parishes, turned out on Christmas
Day and indulged in the game of football with such
vigour that it became little short of a serious fight.*

SIR LAURENCE GOMME (1853–1916), folklore historian
The Village Community

* * * *

'HARK THE HERALD ANGELS SING' WAS WRITTEN IN 1739 BY CHARLES
Wesley, brother of John Wesley, the founder of the Methodist
Church. Many hymns written at that time were just **words without
music**, and it was left to others to choose a tune suitable for the
metre of the verse. Wesley imagined that his 'Hark the Herald' lyrics
would be sung to the same tune as his Easter hymn 'Christ the Lord
Is Risen Today'. The tune we now sing was written by the great
German composer Felix Mendelssohn in 1840 to commemorate the
invention of the printing press by Johannes Gutenberg.

In German churches of the eighteenth century, midnight Christmas services were common, but they were banned in many places because the **congregation was often so drunk and bawdy** that the ceremony descended into chaos and, occasionally, into a mass brawl. Riots used to occur outside the churches before or after the service as crowds of Christmas revellers staggered back and forth from the taverns.

❄ ❄ ❄ ❄

Christmas is so deeply ingrained in our culture today that we can be forgiven for believing that our ancestors celebrated it, in the same way that we do, from the dawn of Christian time. It seems almost incredible that for the better part of two millennia (until the 1840s, roughly) it barely registered as a date of any great significance. Even more remarkable perhaps is the explosive manner of its nineteenth-century revival. Within no more than five to ten years, 25 December went from being a day of **quiet religious observance** for believers to a cultural phenomenon that quickly spread, through an unacknowledged alliance of missionaries and tradesmen, from Britain and America to every corner of the Christian world, and even beyond into other cultures. There were three main catalysts in its dramatic eruption into Victorian society: Charles Dickens, the royal family and a poem by an American, Clement Clark Moore – 'An Account of a Visit from St Nicholas' – which popularized the image of the saint as an overweight, bearded old man in a red suit who traversed the globe in a sleigh pulled by reindeer and delivered gifts down the chimney.

IF ONE EVENT, MORE THAN ANY OTHER, BROUGHT ABOUT THE revitalization of Christmas, while simultaneously reinventing it, it was the publication of Dickens's *A Christmas Carol*. He wrote the tale of Scrooge and Tiny Tim in just two months, finishing it at the end of November 1843. When it was published on 17 December, the book sold out immediately. The themes of charity and goodwill were notions that chimed with the feelings of the middle classes, who were discomfited by the poverty and destitution beyond their cosy homes. **Canny tradesmen** were quick to exploit this sentiment among the burgeoning ranks of Britain's monied classes, and within a decade Christmas had become a highly commercialized event.

❊ ❊ ❊ ❊

The thought of Christmas raises almost automatically the thought of Charles Dickens, and for two very good reasons. To begin with, Dickens is one of the few English writers who have actually written about Christmas … Secondly, Dickens is remarkable, indeed almost unique, among modern writers in being able to give a convincing picture of happiness. Dickens dealt successfully with Christmas twice, in a chapter of The Pickwick Papers *and in* A Christmas Carol. *The latter story was read to Lenin on his deathbed and according to his wife, he found its 'bourgeois sentimentality' completely intolerable. Now in a sense Lenin was right: but if he had been in better health he would perhaps have noticed that the story has interesting sociological implications. To begin with, however thick Dickens may lay on the paint, however disgusting the 'pathos' of Tiny Tim may be, the Cratchit family give the impression of enjoying themselves. They sound happy ... They are in high spirits because for once in a way they have enough to eat. The wolf is at the door, but he is wagging his tail. The steam of the Christmas pudding drifts across a background of pawnshops and sweated labour, and in a double sense the ghost of Scrooge stands beside the dinner table ... The Cratchits are able to enjoy Christmas precisely because it only comes once a year. Their happiness is convincing just because Christmas only comes once a year. Their happiness is convincing just because it is described as incomplete.*

GEORGE ORWELL (1903–50), English Writer
Can Socialists Be Happy?

❄ ❄ ❄ ❄

Happy, happy Christmas, that can win us back to the delusions of our childish days; that can recall to the old man the pleasures of his youth; that can transport the sailor and the traveller, thousands of miles away, back to his own fireside and his quiet home!

CHARLES DICKENS (1812–70)
The Pickwick Papers

CHRISTMAS FOR MOST BRITONS DURING THE INDUSTRIAL REVOLUTION meant just another miserable day of **hard toil** down the mines, or in the mills or fields. It would be decades before ordinary people were able to join the middle classes in a day-long celebration of Christ's Nativity. Many shops continued to open on Christmas Day; bakers baked, tradesmen delivered, postmen posted and miners mined.

❄ ❄ ❄ ❄

At a period of feasts, when the paupers in the Union Workhouses are embraced in the large circle of our sympathies, and cared for a little more liberally than usual, let us draw a circle around the circle, and include within it the beggars in the streets. It may be wrong, as a rule, to encourage street beggars by donations of any kind; but Christmas is an exceptional period and though, possibly, in being charitable to all we may be charitable to many worthless persons, the good Will and good Day will consecrate the deed.

Illustrated London News, December 1848

QUEEN VICTORIA AND HER GERMAN HUSBAND PRINCE ALBERT PLAYED a major part in reviving Christmas. Following their marriage in 1840, Victoria went to great lengths to encourage **German Christmas customs** to make Albert feel at home in Britain. It is thought that it was George III's German consort, Queen Charlotte, who introduced the Christmas tree (*Weihnachtsbaum*) to the British royal family, but it was Albert who made it an institution. Within a year or two, thousands of well-to-do Britons had copied the royals and begun to decorate fir trees in their homes, covering them in candles, toys, handmade cards, strings of candied almonds and small boxes containing gifts and sweets.

❄ ❄ ❄ ❄

'Twas Christmas broach'd the mightiest ale;
'Twas Christmas told the merriest tale;
A Christmas gambol oft could cheer
The poor man's heart through half the year.

SIR WALTER SCOTT (1771–1832), Scottish novelist and poet
Marmion

❄ ❄ ❄ ❄

AS A CHRISTIAN WITH A STRONG SOCIAL CONSCIENCE, VICTORIA WENT to great charitable lengths at Christmas, and the example she set was followed by many others privileged to lead relatively comfortable lives. In 1836, three years before her coronation, she persuaded her mother to send provisions, blankets and coal to a gypsy camp she had visited, writing,

Their being assisted makes me quite merry and happy today, for yesterday night when I was safe and happy at home in that cold night and today when it snowed so and everything looked white, I felt unhappy and grieved to think that our poor gypsy friends should perish and shiver from want.

❄ ❄ ❄ ❄

I must now seek in the children an echo of what Ernest [his brother] and I were in the old time, of what we felt and thought; and their delight in the Christmas-trees is not less than ours used to be.

Prince Albert (1819–60)

❋ ❋ ❋ ❋

At roughly the same time that Victoria, Albert and Dickens – with the help of some profit-hunting tradesmen – were busily restoring and reinventing Christmas in Britain, German settlers in the United States were performing a similar role in the towns and cities of the east coast. German immigrants arrived in America in their tens of thousands in the eighteenth and nineteenth centuries, bringing with them their traditional Christmas customs, and introducing the use of **Christmas trees** to their fellow settlers. For many years, the Christmas period had been something of a drunken and riotous affair in America, occasioning serious outbreaks of disorder, but from the 1830s onwards it rapidly began to evolve into the festival we recognize today, just as it did in England.

IN 1820, THE HIGHLY POPULAR AMERICAN AUTHOR WASHINGTON Irving, under the pseudonym Geoffrey Crayon, published *The Sketch Book*, in which there are long, **colourful, radiant descriptions** of the joyful celebration of Christmas in England. Although Irving had travelled extensively in England, many historians believe that, like Dickens in *A Christmas Carol*, his descriptions were not based on his actual experiences but were pure inventions.

In the course of a December tour in Yorkshire, I rode for a long distance in one of the public coaches, on the day preceding Christmas. The coach was crowded, both inside and out, with passengers, who, by their talk, seemed principally bound to the mansions of relations or friends to eat the Christmas dinner. It was loaded also with hampers of game, and baskets and boxes of delicacies; and hares hung dangling their long ears about the coachman's box — presents from distant friends for the impending feast. I had three fine rosy-cheeked schoolboys for my fellow passengers inside, full of the buxom health and manly spirit which I have observed in the children of this country. They were returning home for the holidays in high glee, and promising themselves a world of enjoyment. It was delightful to hear the gigantic plans of pleasure of the little rogues, and the impracticable feats they were to perform during their six weeks' emancipation from the abhorred thraldom of book, birch, and pedagogue.

WASHINGTON IRVING (1783–1859)
The Sketch Book

Hundreds of silver toned bells of London ring loud, deep and clear from tower and spire to welcome in Christmas. The far-stretching suburbs, like glad children, take up and fling back the sound, over hill and valley, marsh and meadow, while steeple calls to steeple across the winding arms of the mast-covered river, proclaiming to the heathen voyager who has brought his treasures to our coast, and who is ignorant of our religion, the approach of some great Christian festival. Through the long night of departed centuries has that old Saxon sound pealed over our ancient City — from soon after the period when Augustin and his brother monks landed in England, with the banner borne before them, on which was emblazoned the figure of the dying Redeemer, while they moved gravely along, chanting the Holy Litany. We have often paused, with closed eyes, in some star-lighted lane in the suburbs, and listened to the sound of those sweet Christmas bells, until the imagination was borne far away to the fields of Bethlehem (flooded with heavenly light), and we fancied we again heard those angel-voices which startled the shepherds as they watched their flocks by night, while proclaiming high overhead, 'Peace and goodwill towards men.'

THOMAS MILLER (1807–74), poet and author in the Christmas edition of the
Illustrated London News, 1849

❋ ❋ ❋ ❋

'JINGLE BELLS' HAS BEEN A CHRISTMAS FAVOURITE FOR 150 YEARS, BUT it was originally written for the exclusively American celebration of Thanksgiving, which takes place on the last Thursday of November. Its composer, James Pierpoint, called the song 'One Horse Open Sleigh' when he wrote it in 1857, and it proved so popular at Thanksgiving that it was rolled out again a month later at Christmas and has stuck with the December celebration ever since. The song boasts the honour of being the first to be broadcast from space. In December 1965, Gemini 6 astronauts Thomas Stafford and Walter Schirra Jr contacted Mission Control in Houston, allegedly with an important sighting. 'We have an object, looks like a satellite going from north to south, probably in polar orbit,' they reported. 'I see a command module and eight smaller modules in front. The pilot of the command module is wearing a red suit...' The astronauts then took out a harmonica and some sleigh bells and knocked out a fairly ropey rendition of 'Jingle Bells'.

Of late I have been studying with diligence the four prose poems about Christ. At Christmas I managed to get hold of a Greek Testament, and every morning, after I had cleaned my cell and polished my tins, I read a little of the Gospels, a dozen verses taken by chance anywhere. It is a delightful way of opening the day. Every one, even in a turbulent, ill-disciplined life, should do the same. Endless repetition, in and out of season, has spoiled for us the freshness, the naivete, the simple romantic charm of the Gospels. We hear them read far too often and far too badly, and all repetition is anti-spiritual. When one returns to the Greek; it is like going into a garden of lilies out of some narrow and dark house.

OSCAR WILDE (1854–1900)
De Profundis

❋ ❋ ❋ ❋

THOMASING. IN SOME RURAL DISTRICTS THE CUSTOM STILL PREVAILS OF Thomasing – that is, of collecting small sums of money or obtaining drink from the employers of labour on the 21st of December, St Thomas's Day.

Brewer's Dictionary of Phrase and Fable, 1898

❋ ❋ ❋ ❋

There is no more dangerous or disgusting habit than that of celebrating Christmas before it comes, as I am doing in this article. It is the very essence of a festival that it breaks upon one brilliantly and abruptly, that at one moment the great day is not and the next moment the great day is.

G. K. CHESTERTON (1874–1936)
All Things Considered

❋ ❋ ❋ ❋

AT QUEEN VICTORIA'S INSTIGATION, EACH Christmas great quantities of provisions were handed out to the poor of Windsor from the gates of the castle at the top of the town. Among the cartloads of goods were **half a ton of plum puddings**, a ton of bread, vast quantities of beef and potatoes, tons of coal, thousands of blankets and hundreds of cloaks.

Today, Franklin Pierce, the 14th President of the United States, is chiefly remembered for being a tremendous drunk who once ran over a woman in his carriage after necking a bottle or two of strong liquor. On a happier note, perhaps, in 1856 he became the first president to place a **Christmas tree in the White House**. It wasn't until 1923, however, that the presidential tradition of lighting the National Christmas Tree from the White House was initiated — by Calvin Coolidge.

Christmas Day Birthdays

1717 – Pius VI Pope

1642 – Sir Isaac Newton, *mathematician*

1876 – Muhammad Ali Jinnah, *founder of Pakistan*

1878 – Louis Chevrolet, *Swiss-born racing driver*

1891 – Clarrie Grimmett, *Australian cricketer*

1899 – Humphrey Bogart, *American actor*

1907 – Cab Calloway, *American bandleader*

1908 – Quentin Crisp, *English author*

1918 – Anwar Sadat, *President of Egypt*

1945 – Kenny Everett, *English comedian*

1949 – Sissy Spacek, *American actress*

1954 – Annie Lennox, *Scottish singer*

1957 – Shane McGowan, *Irish singer*

1971 – Dido Florian Cloud de Bounevialle Armstrong, *aka Dido, English singer*

Christmas Day Deaths

795 – Pope Adrian I

1156 – Peter the Venerable, *Benedictine abbot of Cluny*

1926 – Yoshihito, *Emperor of Japan*

1938 – Karel Čapek, *Czech author*

1946 – W. C. Fields, *American comedian*

1977 – Charlie Chaplin, *English actor*

1983 – Joan Miró, *Catalan painter*

1989 – Nicolae Ceauşescu, *Romanian dictator*

1995 – Dean Martin, *American singer*

2006 – James Brown, *American singer*

The fir tree was put into a great tub filled with sand ... The servants, and the young ladies also decked it out. On one branch they hung little nets, cut out of coloured paper; every net was filled with sweetmeats; golden apples and walnuts hung down as if they grew there, and more than a hundred little candles, red, white and blue, were fastened to the different boughs. Dolls that looked exactly like real people — the Tree had never seen such before — swung among the foliage, and high on the summit of the Tree was fixed a tinsel star. It was splendid, particularly splendid. 'This evening,' said all. 'This evening it will shine.'

HANS CHRISTIAN ANDERSEN (1805–75)
The Fir Tree

✳ ✳ ✳ ✳

IT WAS DURING THE VICTORIAN PERIOD THAT THE **PANTOMIME**, based on the Italian travelling 'harlequinades' of the previous century, began to evolve into the kitsch, slapstick productions we recognize today. The Victorians loved the pantomime, and the shows during that time became increasingly spectacular and innovative as rival theatre owners vied with each other to put on the best show of the season. A great deal of mechanical ingenuity was needed to pull off a number of special effects, such as flying devices and trapdoors, while some theatres even installed giant water tanks below the stage to create water features like waterfalls, rivers and even sea battles. Pantomime was not to everyone's taste, however ...

I am sorry to have to introduce the subject of Christmas ... It is an indecent subject; a cruel, gluttonous subject; a wicked, cadging, lying, filthy, blasphemous, and demoralizing subject. Christmas is forced on a reluctant and disgusted nation by the shopkeepers and the press: on its own merits it would wither and shrivel in the fiery breath of universal hatred; and anyone who looked back to it would be turned into a pillar of greasy sausages. Yet, though it is over now for a year, and I can go out without positively elbowing my way through the groves of carcasses, I am dragged back to it, with my soul full of loathing, by the pantomime.

GEORGE BERNARD SHAW (1856–1950), Irish dramatist and essayist
Our Theatres in the Nineties, **1898**

BY THE END OF THE NINETEENTH CENTURY, THE CRYSTAL PALACE, relocated to Sydenham from Hyde Park after the Great Exhibition of 1851, was staging a Christmas Variety extravaganza, which the organizers billed as 'The Finest, Most Costly and Most Varied Christmas Show in Europe!' A series of spectacular entertainments included foreign circus performers, Bedouin Arabs showing off their equestrian prowess, Japanese high-wire performers, tumbling clowns and even a pair of **high-diving horses** from the United States. The thoroughbreds ran up a fenced-off walkway before leaping headfirst into a pool of water.

DEC. 19 – JAN. 31

Bertram

MILLS CIRCUS

OLYMPIA   Grand Hall

TWICE DAILY
2·30 & 7 p.m.

★ 3 SHOWS ★
DEC. 26 (Boxing Day)
and every Saturday
1·45 p.m. 5 p.m. 8·15 p.m.

Visit the
FUN FAIR
Open noon daily

over 500 unreserved seats at each performance

THERE ARE **TWO CHRISTMAS ISLANDS**. ONE IS IN THE INDIAN OCEAN and acquired its name after it was sighted on that day in 1643 by Captain William Mynors of the British East India Company aboard the *Royal Mary*. It has a population of 1,500 and is administered by Australia. Not much happens there apart from a spot of phosphate mining. In spite of its name, only about 15 per cent of the people are Christian, the rest being mainly Buddhist or Muslim. The other Christmas Island, in the Micronesia region of the Pacific Ocean, was discovered by Captain Cook on Christmas Eve, 1777. The island, which gained its independence as part of Kiribati in 1979, is the largest and oldest atoll in the world, but that didn't stop the British carrying out nuclear tests there in the 1950s.

THE CHRISTMAS ROYAL MESSAGE WAS STARTED BY KING GEORGE V IN 1932, when he spoke to the Empire over the 'wireless' from his study in his Norfolk home of Sandringham. The text, featuring just 251 words, was written by Rudyard Kipling. Using a microphone encased in Australian walnut, the king advised his subjects to work for peace and for 'prosperity without self-seeking'. He concluded the address thus:

My life's aim has been to serve as I might towards those ends. Your loyalty, your confidence in me, has been my abundant reward. I speak now from my home and my heart to you all; to men and women so cut off by the snows, the desert or the sea that only voices out of the air can reach them; to those cut off from fuller life by blindness, sickness or infirmity, and to those who are celebrating this day with their children and their grandchildren — to all, to each, I wish a happy Christmas. God bless you.

❋ ❋ ❋ ❋

CHRISTMAS, A TOWN IN ORANGE COUNTY, FLORIDA, IS THEMED ON the festive day from which it took its name. Amongst the attractions at the town's Jungle Adventures recreation park is a **200-foot-long replica of an alligator**. Christmas is just one of several places with names that recall the winter holiday season. In Alaska, you will find the town of North Pole; in Georgia and Indiana there are towns called Santa Claus; Noel in Missouri; Rudolph in Wisconsin; Snowflake in Arizona and Dasher in Georgia.

SINCE 1864 MEMBERS OF THE SERPENTINE SWIMMING CLUB HAVE MET in London's Hyde Park every Christmas morning to **race across the icy lake**. For forty years the winner of the 100-yard dash was awarded a gold medal, but in 1904 writer Sir James Barrie, a patron of the race, presented the first Peter Pan Cup, which was named after his most famous character.

✳ ✳ ✳ ✳

'SILENT NIGHT', THE world's most popular carol, was supposedly dashed off in a couple of hours by Austrian priest Joseph Mohr. The legend goes that a few hours before Mohr was due to conduct Midnight Mass, the organ at St Nicholas's Church in the Alpine village of Oberndorf broke down. Mohr hastily set about writing a three-stanza carol that could be sung with just a choir or a guitar, and later that evening the strains of '*Stille Nacht*' were heard for the first time.

✳ ✳ ✳ ✳

We consider Christmas as the encounter, the great encounter, the historical encounter, the decisive encounter, between God and mankind. He who has faith knows this truly; let him rejoice.

POPE PAUL VI (1897–1978)

✳ ✳ ✳ ✳

There is a remarkable breakdown of taste and intelligence at Christmas-time. Mature, responsible grown men wear neckties made of holly leaves and drink alcoholic beverages with raw egg yolks and cottage cheese in them.

P. J. O'ROURKE (1947–)
American humorist

THE SURGEON

THE ROADS WERE VERY QUIET WHEN I DROVE BACK TO QUEEN Alexandra Hospital in Portsmouth on Christmas morning to check on a patient I had operated on 12 hours earlier. I imagined I would only be there for a short while, and would be back in time to join my family for the church service up in the little chapel across the fields.

After parking the car, I decided to take the short cut up to the ward through A&E. I remember feeling a little self-conscious as I walked through the doors because I was wearing my new Christmas jumper. It all seemed very quiet, almost eerie. As I strode through I noticed someone having cardiac massage in 'resuss' (the resuscitation area). For some reason, it struck me as quite a surreal sight, perhaps because this battle for life was taking place in an otherwise very still and very quiet atmosphere. Usually, A&E is a bustle of noise and activity.

As I walked into the main workstation area, there were two surgical registrars talking together, which is not something you expect to see early on Christmas Day morning. I knew something was up because they were both accountable to me, and my first thought was that there had been some complications with the patient on whom I'd operated the night before.

'Ah, Mr Pemberton, we were just trying to call you,' one of them said. 'We might have a ruptured aortic aneurysm for you. Did you see that man in A&E?'

I was a little surprised to hear this, sceptical even, because it's very rare that someone who suffers such a rupture survives long enough for cardiac massage to be performed.

I went straight back to resuss, and the patient was looking pretty clapped out as the cardiac team continued to work on him. Whenever they stopped he had no blood pressure, and the consensus was that he was too far gone to be saved. Any further efforts seemed futile, so once we had established that as a certainty I turned to his wife to explain what was happening and give her the bad news. It felt very odd. A minute or two earlier I had been whistling my way across the car park, looking forward to having a chat with the patients on the wards, and the next thing I knew I was telling a woman her husband was about to die. 'Hello, I'm the duty vascular surgeon,' I heard myself say. 'Your husband is having cardiac massage.' I explained to her as best I could what a ruptured aneurysm meant and then said: 'It seems highly likely he's about to die, whatever we do, and these are the options: though his chances of survival are very slim indeed we can take him to the operating theatre, or we accept that unfortunately he's too far gone and sadly we have missed the very small window of opportunity we had to save him.'

'I want you to try and save him, even if it seems impossible,' she replied. Seconds later I was tearing off my Christmas jumper and quickly putting on my surgical clothes. We all rushed into the theatre, even though I was expecting someone to come in at any moment to tell me that the patient had passed away. I was absolutely stunned when he was wheeled in and I was told he still had a pulse, albeit a weak one.

We covered his chest in antiseptic, put on some drapes and, no more than two or three minutes after talking to his wife, I was cutting the man open from his sternum to his pubis and clamping his aorta just above the diseased segment that had burst. That done, there was a brief respite while the anaesthetic team improved his general condition by giving him more fluids and stabilizing his blood pressure. This is a great moment because if the patient's still alive when you clamp them, you know they're in with a chance. We had to use an awful lot of blood throughout the operation because, as is the case with patients in shock, his blood wouldn't clot and everything we stitched just carried on bleeding until the coagulant products eventually started to work their magic. The human body contains an average of eight units of blood, and we used about 30 in this operation, which is masses.

We spent a full four hours repairing the rupture but as the operation wore on I grew in confidence that he was going to make it. It was an exciting feeling, knowing that this man was coming back from the brink. Somehow, the fact that it was Christmas Day made it all the more thrilling.

It was the middle of the afternoon by the time we were done and the man could be wheeled out of the theatre to one of the wards. I was still buzzing with excitement when I finally arrived home – just in time to carve the giant turkey and pour the wine for our guests. In the event, our man made a full recovery, was back home two weeks later, and at the time of writing he's still alive, over four years on. It wasn't quite a miracle, but it wasn't far off. Not since I was a young child have I felt the spirit of Christmas so keenly as I did that day in 2002.

MARK PEMBERTON, vascular surgeon

Elephants on the Thames:

Christmas Weather

WE DON'T BAT AN EYELID WHEN WE RECEIVE CHRISTMAS CARDS depicting the Holy Land waist-deep in snow, with cartoon images of shepherds tobogganing, wise men throwing snowballs at each other and reindeer ice-skating on the Sea of Galilee. Such wintry images have become so commonplace that we have ceased to be moved by their absurdity. It's a little odd, though, that snow and ice have somehow crept into the Nativity picture when you consider that the average temperature in the Bethlehem region in late December is about 11 degrees centigrade, with a seasonal high of around 15 degrees. Normally when temperatures soar to these heights in Britain outside summer, people fling open their windows, strip off their tops, fire up the barbie and start exclaiming: 'Well, if this is global warming then BRING! IT! ON!' **Jesus may well have seen some snow** in his lifetime because it does occasionally fall in the Holy Land, but rarely to great depths and by and large only on the highest peaks. Dickens provides the answer to the anomaly. When he was writing his many snow-sprinkled tales about Christmas, Britain was still in the thick of what meteorologists call a 'mini Ice Age', which ran from roughly the mid-fifteenth to the mid-nineteenth century. During that period, winters were much colder than they are today and some of them were so severe that there was sea ice around the British coastline. Dickens's descriptions of frozen winters and white Christmases have stuck in the popular imagination, blanketing every aspect of the holiday period with a scattering of snow – even the Middle East.

✻ ✻ ✻ ✻

DURING BRITAIN'S MINI ICE AGE (C. 1450 TO 1850) THE **THAMES froze over** on many occasions, often for weeks on end, and occasionally for months, as in the case of the 'Great Winters' of 1683/84 and 1715/16. There are a number of reasons why the river iced over so frequently, in addition to the fact that it was much colder than it is today. The Thames was much wider and shallower in those days, which meant it flowed far more slowly – conditions which make a river more susceptible to freezing. In the mid-nineteenth century the great engineer Sir Joseph Bazalgette narrowed the Thames appreciably as part of his remarkable reconstruction of London's sewage system. By building embankments out into the river, he increased the speed of its flow. (Chelsea Embankment alone reclaimed 52 acres of land.) The old London Bridge, with its 19 narrow arches restricting the river's flow, was another factor. The bridge was replaced in 1831 with John Rennie's new design, which has far wider arches.

✻ ✻ ✻ ✻

IN THE WINTER OF 1536, HENRY VIII TRAVELLED FROM WESTMINSTER to Greenwich by sleigh along the frozen Thames. The chronicler Raphael Holinshed described a severe cold snap over the Christmas period in 1564:

On New Year's even, people went over and along the Thames on the ice from London Bridge to Westminster. Some played at the foot-ball as boldly there as if it had been on dry land ... the people, both men and women, went daily on the Thames in greater number than in any street of the city of London. On the 3rd day of January it began to thaw, and on the 5th day was no ice to be seen between London Bridge and Lambeth; which sudden thaw caused great floods and high waters, that bare down bridges and houses, and drowned many people, especially in Yorkshire.

ALTHOUGH WE KNOW THE THAMES HAD FROZEN OVER ON A NUMBER of occasions in the preceding 200 years or so, there is no record of a '**frost fair**' until 1608. Compared to later fairs, this was a rudimentary effort with a few tents and food stalls and an area set aside for ice bowling. The winter of 1607/8 was so severe that trees died of frost and ships were icebound several miles out into the frozen North Sea.

✻ ✻ ✻ ✻

Now trees their leafy hats do bare,
To reverence Winter's silver hair;
A handsome hostess, merry host,
A pot of ale now and a toast,
Tobacco and a good coal fire,
Are things this season doth require.
Poor Robin's Almanack, 1684

✻ ✻ ✻ ✻

IN THE WINTER OF 1683/84, CONSIDERED TO BE THE COLDEST IN Britain's history, the Thames began to freeze over in mid-December and it was solid from Middlesex to London Bridge by the turn of the year. It remained frozen for eight weeks and the ice was almost two foot thick in some places. English diarist John Evelyn described the sprawling frost fair that took place that year:

The frost continuing, more and more severe, the Thames, before London, was still planted with booths in formal streets, all sorts of trades and shops, furnished and full of commodities, even to a printing press, where the people and ladies took a fancy to have their names printed, and the day and the year set down when produced on the Thames: ... Coaches plied from Westminster to the Temple and from other stairs, to and fro, as in the streets; sleds, sliding with skates, or bull-baiting, horse and coach races, puppet-shows and interludes, cooks, tippling and other lewd places; so that it seemed to be a bacchanalian triumph or carnival on the water: while it was a severe judgment on the land, the trees not only splitting as if lightning-struck, but men and cattle perishing in divers places, and the very seas so locked up with ice, that no vessels could stir out or come in; the fowls, fish, and birds, and all our exotic plants and greens, universally perishing. Many parks of deer were destroyed; and all sorts of fuel so dear, that there were great contributions to keep the poor alive ... London, by reason of the excessive coldness of the air hindering the ascent of the smoke, was so filled with the fuliginous stream of the sea-coal, that hardly could any one see across the streets; and this filling of the lungs with the gross particles exceedingly obstructed the breath, so as one could scarcely breathe. There was no water to be had from the pipes or engines; nor could the brewers and divers other tradesmen work; and every moment was full of disastrous accidents.

THE WINTER OF 1694/95 WAS ALMOST AS COLD AS THE ONE 11 YEARS earlier and the snow and ice which bound up the country in December didn't loosen its grip until a big thaw in the middle of April. The weather was so severe that sea ice in the Arctic extended so far south that it wrapped around the entire coastline of Iceland. In 1715/16, there was another frost fair as the Thames froze for two months. The ice was so thick and solid that it didn't break when a flood tide raised the water levels below by about 10 feet.

THE TIDAL STRETCH OF THE THAMES FROZE FOR THE LAST TIME IN THE winter of 1813/14, which ranks in the top five of Britain's harshest and snowiest winters. The huge blocks of ice that floated down the river as it began to thaw and break caused extensive damage to ships. Travelling around the country was virtually impossible as canals and rivers froze over and roads became impassable in many places. A frost fair was held on the Thames. Though it lasted only four days it is described as one of the most spectacular of them all, featuring a high street, named City Road, running down the middle of the river, rather than across it as in earlier years. Visitors flocked to the fair in their thousands to enjoy the entertainment, which included merry-go-rounds, theatrical shows, 'street' performers, donkey rides, swings, skittles and dancing-booths. A huge crowd gathered on Blackfriars Bridge and on the river itself when Londoners, for the first and last time, were treated to the bizarre sight of an **elephant sliding its way** from one side of the river to the other.

❋ ❋ ❋ ❋

There was glittering in the atmosphere, as if it was filled with innumerable shining particles; and the noble bay horses that drew the sleigh were covered, in many parts, with a coat of hoar-frost. The vapor from their nostrils was seen to issue like smoke; and every object in the view, as well as every arrangement of the travellers, denoted the depth of a winter in the mountains. The harness, which was of a deep, dull black, differing from the glossy varnishing of the present day, was ornamented with enormous plates and buckles of brass, that shone like gold in those transient beams of the sun which found their way obliquely through the tops of the trees. Huge saddles, studded with nails and fitted with cloth that served as blankets to the shoulders of the cattle, supported four high, square-topped turrets, through which the stout reins led from the mouths of the horses to the hands of the driver, who was a negro, of apparently twenty years of age. His face, which nature had colored with a glistening black, was now mottled with the cold, and his large shining eyes filled with tears; a tribute to its power that the keen frosts of those regions always extracted from one of his African origin. Still, there was a smiling expression of good-humor in his happy countenance, that was created by the thoughts of home and a Christmas fireside, with its Christmas frolics.

JAMES FENIMORE COOPER (1789–1851), American writer
The Pioneers

December 21st. Great black clouds were rolling across the heavens, and squalls of rain, with hail, swept by us with such extreme violence, that the Captain determined to run into Wigwam Cove. This is a snug little harbour, not far from Cape Horn; and here, at Christmas-eve, we anchored in smooth water. The only thing which reminded us of the gale outside, was every now and then a puff from the mountains, which made the ship surge at her anchors.

CHARLES DARWIN (1809–82), English naturalist
The Voyage of the Beagle

❄ ❄ ❄ ❄

BRITAIN WAS BLANKETED IN DEEP SNOW OVER THE CHRISTMAS PERIOD of 1836, inspiring Charles Dickens's wintry Christmases in *The Pickwick Papers* and *A Christmas Carol*. It's strange to think that had it not been for a quirk of the northern hemisphere climate in December of that year, the association of Christmas with heavy snow would, in all probability, never have taken hold in British culture and our sense of Christmas today would be entirely different. The Christmas Day snow of 1836 was truly remarkable even by the standards of that colder age. It was said to have been over 12 feet deep in some parts of the country, with drifts of 20 to 30 feet. The heavy falls made all but a few roads impassable and they also triggered **Britain's deadliest avalanche**, which claimed the lives of eight people when it demolished two homes in Lewes, East Sussex. A pub in the town called the Snowdrop was named after the disaster.

On Saturday last the earth was frostbound, on Sunday night it rained violently, and on Christmas-eve the roads and pathways, especially in the suburbs of London, were converted into a hopeless slough of despond; indeed, a most miserable, dark, damp, dismal, and depressing day than Tuesday it has seldom been our fate to behold even in December. The sun, as if ashamed not to show his face on Christmas day, did shine, for a brief space between one and two o'clock, but clouds soon obscured the sky, and darkness visible prevailed till the shutters were closed, and the Christmas candles lent their artificial light. Yet the traffic in the streets was immense. To obtain a seat in an omnibus, penny or sixpenny, was out of the question, unless the rash traveller was content to sit on the 'knifeboard', exposed to the rain and wind, and likely to contract a catarrh to last him his life. All the public vehicles were crammed, and the pedestrians on the footways were often jostled by the crowds that, bent on exercise, or about to 'visit the relations', contentedly waded through the slush which defiled the pavements. Many of the shops, not forgetting the druggists', were open, and attracted the gaze, if not the money, of the passers-by. Those useful members of society, the red-coated shoeblacks, had their hands full of business, and the cry of 'Clean your boots?' was assuredly not raised in vain.

Illustrated London News, 29 December 1855

❄ ❄ ❄ ❄

Fine old Christmas, with the snowy hair and ruddy face, had done his duty that year in the noblest fashion, and had set off his rich gifts of warmth and colour with all the heightening contrast of frost and snow. Snow lay on the croft and river-bank in undulations softer than the limbs of infancy; it lay with the neatliest finished border on every sloping roof, making the dark-red gables stand out with a new depth of colour; it weighed heavily on the laurels and fir-trees, till it fell from them with a shuddering sound; it clothed the rough turnip-field with whiteness, and made the sheep look like dark blotches; the gates were all blocked up with the sloping drifts, and here and there a disregarded four-footed beast stood as if petrified 'in unrecumbent sadness'; there was no gleam, no shadow, for the heavens, too, were one still, pale cloud; no sound or motion in anything but the dark river that flowed and moaned like an unresting sorrow. But old Christmas smiled as he laid this cruel-seeming spell on the outdoor world, for he meant to light up home with new brightness, to deepen all the richness of indoor colour, and give a keener edge of delight to the warm fragrance of food; he meant to prepare a sweet imprisonment that would strengthen the primitive fellowship of kindred, and make the sunshine of familiar human faces as welcome as the hidden day-star.

GEORGE ELIOT (1819–80), English novelist
The Mill on the Floss

The time draws near the birth of Christ:
The moon is hid; the night is still;
The Christmas bells from hill to hill
Answer each other in the mist

ALFRED, LORD TENNYSON (1809–92), English poet
from 'In Memoriam A. H. H.'

❄ ❄ ❄ ❄

A protracted frost necessarily deranges the lower class of employments in such a city as London, and throws many poor persons into destitution. Just as sure as this is the fact... that a vast horde of the class who systematically avoid regular work, preferring to live by their wits, simulate the characteristic appearances of distressed labourers, and try to excite the charity of the better class of citizens. Investing themselves in aprons, clutching an old spade, and hoisting as their signal of distress a turnip on the top of a pole or rake, they will wend their way through the west-end streets, proclaiming themselves in sepulchral tones as Frozen-out Gardeners, or simply calling, 'Hall frozen hout!' or chanting 'We've got no work to do.' The faces of the corps are duly dolorous; but one can nevertheless observe a sharp eye kept on the doors and windows they are passing, in order that if possible they may arrest some female gaze on which to practise their spell of pity. It is alleged on good grounds that the generality of these victims of the frost are impostors, and that their daily gatherings will often amount to double a skilled workman's wages. Nor do they usually discontinue the trade till long after the return of milder airs has liquidated even real claims upon the public sympathy.

ROBERT CHAMBERS (1802–71)
Chambers Book of Days

Dear Dolly:

I wish you a merry Christmas, and want you to buy whatever you think you would like with the enclosed check for twenty dollars. It is now just forty years since you stopped being my nurse, when I was a little boy of seven, just one year younger than Quentin now is. I wish you could see the children play here in the White House grounds. For the last three days there has been snow, and Archie and Quentin and their cousin, cunning little Sheffield Cowles, and their other cousin, Mr. John Elliott's little girl, Helena, who is a perfect little dear, have been having all kinds of romps in the snow — coasting, having snowball fights, and doing everything — in the grounds back of the White House. This coming Saturday afternoon I have agreed to have a great play of hide-and-go-seek in the White House itself, not only with these children but with their various small friends.

THEODORE ROOSEVELT (1858–1919), letter to his old nurse, Mrs Dora Watkins,
from the White House, 19 December 1905

❊ ❊ ❊ ❊

THE **HEAVIEST SNOW IN ENGLAND** ON CHRISTMAS DAY WAS RECORDED in 1927, when a blizzard swept from the Midlands across the south as far as Cornwall. Most places woke up on Boxing Day morning to find several feet of snow outside their front door and many villages were cut off. The drifts in the Chilterns were 20 feet deep and up to 25 feet deep across Salisbury Plain. Aeroplanes dropped supplies to remote villages as the BBC issued instructions over the wireless to lay out shapes of dark clothes to help the pilots.

❊ ❊ ❊ ❊

It was on the afternoon of the Christmas Eve, and I was in Mrs. Prothero's garden, waiting for cats, with her son Jim. It was snowing. It was always snowing at Christmas. December, in my memory, is white as Lapland, though there were no reindeers. But there were cats. Patient, cold and callous, our hands wrapped in socks, we waited to snowball the cats. Sleek and long as jaguars and horrible-whiskered, spitting and snarling, they would slink and sidle over the white back-garden walls, and the lynx-eyed hunters, Jim and I, fur-capped and moccasined

trappers from Hudson Bay, off Mumbles Road, would hurl our deadly snowballs at the green of their eyes. The wise cats never appeared ... Years and years ago, when I was a boy, when there were wolves in Wales, and birds the colour of red-flannel petticoats whisked past the harp-shaped hills, when we sang and wallowed all night and day in caves that smelt like Sunday afternoons in damp front farmhouse parlours, and we chased, with the jawbones of deacons, the English and the bears, before the motor car, before the wheel, before the duchess-faced horse, when we rode the daft and happy hills bareback, it snowed and it snowed. But here a small boy says: 'It snowed last year, too. I made a snowman and my brother knocked it down and I knocked my brother down and then we had tea.'

'But that was not the same snow,' I say. 'Our snow was not only shaken from white wash buckets down the sky, it came shawling out of the ground and swam and drifted out of the arms and hands and bodies of the trees; snow grew overnight on the roofs of the houses like a pure and grandfather moss, minutely ivied the walls and settled on the postman, opening the gate, like a dumb, numb thunder-storm of white, torn Christmas cards.'

DYLAN THOMAS (1914–53), Welsh poet
A Child's Christmas in Wales

❄ ❄ ❄ ❄

Monday 25 December [1912]

The wind was strong last night and this morning; a light snowfall in the night and this morning; a good deal of drift, subsiding when we started, but still about a foot high ... I must write a word of our supper last night. We had four courses. The first, pemmican, full whack, with slices of horse meat flavoured with onion and curry powder and thickened with biscuit; then an arrowroot, cocoa and biscuit hoosh sweetened; then a plum pudding; then cocoa with raisins, and finally a dessert of caramels and ginger. After the feast it was difficult to move. Wilson and I couldn't finish our share of plum pudding. We have all slept splendidly and feel thoroughly warm — such is the effect of full feeding.

ROBERT FALCON SCOTT (1868–1912)
Scott's Last Expedition: The Journals

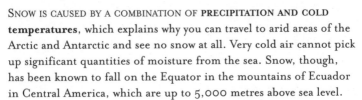

SNOW IS CAUSED BY A COMBINATION OF **PRECIPITATION AND COLD temperatures**, which explains why you can travel to arid areas of the Arctic and Antarctic and see no snow at all. Very cold air cannot pick up significant quantities of moisture from the sea. Snow, though, has been known to fall on the Equator in the mountains of Ecuador in Central America, which are up to 5,000 metres above sea level.

❇ ❇ ❇ ❇

'I'M DREAMING OF A WHITE CHRISTMAS', WRITTEN BY IRVING BERLIN and sung by Bing Crosby, took just 18 minutes to record in 1942. The Crosby version, which featured in the film *Holiday Inn*, has sold over 50 million copies worldwide and until 1997 it was the bestselling single of all time. It is the only song to have gone to the **top of the US charts** on three different occasions.

❇ ❇ ❇ ❇

We grouped ourselves round the farmhouse porch. The sky cleared and broad streams of stars ran down over the valley and away to Wales. On Slad's white slopes, seen through the black sticks of its woods, some red lamps burned in the windows.

Everything was quiet: everywhere there was the faint crackling silence of the winter night. We started singing, and we were all moved by the words and the sudden trueness of our voices. Pure, very clear, and breathless we sang:

*'As Joseph was walking
He heard an angel sing;
"This night shall be the birth-time
Of Christ the Heavenly King.
He neither shall be bored
In house nor in hall
Not in a place of paradise
But in an ox's stall …"'*

And two thousand Christmases became real to us then; the houses, the halls, the places of paradise had all been visited; the stars were bright to guide the Kings through the snow; and across the farmyard we could hear the beasts in their stalls. We were given roast apples and hot mince pies, in our nostrils were spices like myrrh, and in our wooden box, as we headed back for the village, there were golden gifts for all.

LAURIE LEE (1914–97), **English writer**
Cider with Rosie

At Christmas I no more desire a rose
Than wish a snow in May's new-fangled mirth;
But like of each thing that in season grows.

WILLIAM SHAKESPEARE
Love's Labour's Lost

❄ ❄ ❄ ❄

For many people, indeed, the charm of
Christmas is inseparably associated with the
country; it is lost in London — the city is too
vast, too modern, too sophisticated. It is bound
up with the thought of frosty fields, of bells heard
far away, of bare trees against the starlit sky,
of carols sung not by trained choirs but by rustic
folk with rough accent, irregular time, and tunes
learnt by ear and not by book.

CLEMENT A. MILES
Christmas Customs and Traditions, **1912**

❄ ❄ ❄ ❄

Christmas came and except for the ceremonial Mass, the
solemn and wearisome Christmas congratulations from
neighbours and servants, and the new dresses everyone
put on, there were no special festivities, though the calm
frost of twenty degrees Reaumur, the dazzling sunshine by
day, and the starlight of the winter nights seemed to call
for some special celebration of the season.

LEO TOLSTOY
War and Peace, **1863–9**

❄ ❄ ❄ ❄

WE HAVE BECOME SO DESPERATE TO FULFIL OUR ANNUAL DREAM OF
a white Christmas that the official definition of one — created
by bookmakers — is the falling of **just one flake** on the roof of the
London Weather Centre within the 24 hours of 25 December.
The last time a proper blanket of snow descended on the capital
on Christmas Day was in 1895. Statistics show that Britain is just
as likely to experience a white Easter as it is a white Christmas.

IN THE TWENTIETH CENTURY, SNOW FELL OVER LONDON ON
Christmas Day on 10 occasions: 1916, 1927, 1938,
1956, 1964, 1968, 1970, 1976, 1996 and 1999. The
snow lay on the ground in 1927, 1938 and 1970 – but
1981 was also 'white', owing to earlier falls. Strangely, in
spite of climate change bringing higher average temperatures,
widespread sleet/snow fell across large areas of the UK on
five Christmases between 1993 and 2003, whereas it did
so only once, in 1980, between 1971 and 1992. Snow over
the high ground of Scotland is far more common, but in
Glasgow it has fallen on 25 December just 10 times since
1918. Unless you happen to be a Lake District goatherd, you
are very unlikely to experience a white Christmas in the UK
in the twenty-first century as the planet continues to warm
up. Recent research suggests that our Christmases are going
to be **very wet and very warm** in the years to come, posing
interesting conundrums for our Christmas card illustrators. Do
they keep trotting out the white Christmas nonsense? Or will a
grittier realism win the day and we'll all start sending each other
cards carrying images of Donner and Blitzen being swept away in
flash floods and Mary and the baby Jesus being winched to the
safety of a Sea King helicopter from the rooftop of their stable?

❄ ❄ ❄ ❄

A FEW MONTHS AFTER THE SECOND WORLD WAR BROKE OUT, THE
British suffered their harshest winter for 50 years. The cold snap
began over Christmas as a hard frost and fog enveloped the country.
In January, the wintry weather brought much of Britain to an ice-
bound standstill, hampering the war effort and adding to the mood
of **national gloom** (unless you were a seven-year-old with a
toboggan or a pair of skates). The Thames froze for eight
miles at the beginning of the non-tidal stretch between

Teddington and Sunbury, while ice also covered lengths of the Mersey, Humber and Severn. The sea froze at Bognor Regis and the harbours at Folkestone and Southampton, further along the south coast, iced over. The 140-mile-long Grand Union Canal between Birmingham and London was frozen solid.

❄ ❄ ❄ ❄

TWO YEARS SHARE THE RECORD FOR THE **WARMEST CHRISTMAS DAY** since records began: 1896, when the temperature reached 15.6 Centigrade (60F) in Leith, near Edinburgh, and 1920, when the same level was recorded in Killerton, Devon.

10 winter-flowering plants

Cornus alba '*Elegantissima*'

Chimonanthus praecox

Berberis thunbergii atropurpurea '*Rose Glow*'

Viburnum x bodnantense 'Deben'

Clematis cirrhosa var. balearica

Sarcococca hookeriana var. digyna

Abeliophyllum distichum

Mahonia japonica '*Bealei*'

Chaenomeles x superba '*Coral Sea*'

Ilex x altaclerensis '*Golden King*'

ALTHOUGH TEMPERATURES WERE GENERALLY MUCH COLDER THAN today, there is another reason why there was a greater chance of snow at Christmas in days gone by, or at least until 1752. It was in that year that Britain finally followed the lead of the Catholic countries and **switched from the Julian to the Gregorian calendar**. On the night of the switch, Britain went to bed on 2 September and woke up on 14 September. Until the change, Christmas Day had been celebrated on our equivalent of 6 January, 12 days deeper into winter.

❄ ❄ ❄ ❄

THE WINTER OF 1947 WAS **ONE OF THE HARSHEST** EVER EXPERIENCED in Britain, but it didn't arrive until the end of January after an unseasonably mild period when temperatures rose to 15 degrees Centigrade in parts of the country. From 22 January to 17 March, however, snow fell every day somewhere in Britain (even in the Scilly Isles) and it accumulated very quickly, causing drifts of up to 15 feet that blocked many roads, major and minor, and brought the railways to a halt.

THE WINTER OF 1962/63, ONE OF THE COLDEST AND SNOWIEST IN British history, brought the country to a virtual standstill for days and even weeks on end. Almost the entire country lay frozen solid under a thick pile of snow and ice for the better part of three months. It began in Scotland just before Christmas, when heavy rain turned to snow, and then headed down to England, where it came to a stop over the Home Counties and carpeted the region under an expanse of white. Even the Channel Islanders awoke to find a foot of snow. It was still on the ground when a blizzard swept across south-west England and Wales on 29 and 30 December, creating drifts up to 20 feet deep, paralysing transport routes, isolating hundreds of villages and cutting off power to tens of thousands of homes. The temperatures then crashed (it was minus 16 degrees in Gatwick, and minus 22 in Braemar, Scotland) and the country turned into a giant ice block. Many rivers (including non-tidal stretches of the Thames) froze up and even the **sea iced over** around the coasts, up to half a mile out in some places. In a throwback to Tudor and Stuart times, ice floes could be seen floating along the Thames in central London. Thousands of sheep, cattle and horses starved because farmers were unable to get food to them through the drifts. Millions of wild birds were killed by the freezing temperatures and a lack of food. Throughout the winter, though, there was plenty of sunshine, turning the whole of Britain into a giant spectacular winter landscape.

❄ ❄ ❄ ❄

AMERICAN METEOROLOGISTS AT THE NATIONAL Climatic Data Center have calculated the **probability** of American cities experiencing a white Christmas, based on twentieth-century data, and using one inch of snow on the ground as the definition of 'white'. It probably came as little surprise to the ice-bound people of Marquette (Michigan) that they can guarantee one every year, scoring 100 per cent probability. Anchorage

(Alaska) scored the next best chance of a white Christmas with 90 per cent, followed by Concord (New Hampshire) on 87 per cent and Fargo (South Dakota) and Portland (Maine) on 83 per cent. New York and Philadelphia have just a 10 per cent chance, Boston 23 per cent, Detroit and Denver 50 per cent, Chicago 40 per cent, and Seattle a miserable 7 per cent. Los Angeles, San Francisco, Phoenix (Arizona), Miami, Charlotte (North Carolina), Portland (Oregon) and Dallas have precisely no chance.

❄ ❄ ❄ ❄

SNOWMEN ARE NOT A MODERN INVENTION. Historians of pagan culture believe our ancestors used to build them in order to ward off evil winter spirits. They can only be built with packing snow, i.e. snow that is close to melting. The **largest snowman ever** was made in Maine, USA, in 1999. 'Angus' measured 35 metres high. Then he melted.

❄ ❄ ❄ ❄

SNOWFLAKES REMAIN ONE OF THE GREAT MYSTERIES OF NATURE AS scientists have yet to explain *exactly* how they come to acquire their unique shapes. What we do know is that flakes form when water in the atmosphere is cooled below its freezing point, entering a 'supercooled' state. The flakes then develop around minuscule dust particles in the air – which act as nuclei for condensation – and then form in the shape of a hexagon with an infinite number of variations. (The reason they are always six-sided is not as interesting as you may think. Trust me, it's to do with the atomic structure of water.) The shapes of the ice crystals are influenced by the temperature and humidity of the air, but collisions with other flakes and partial melting will also alter their form. It is accepted as fact that **no two snowflakes are exactly the same**, but this can never be officially proven, owing to the obvious impossibility of analysing every flake that falls from the sky. The widespread belief that all snowflakes are symmetrical is mistaken. In fact, only 1 per cent of them are truly symmetrical. The most elaborate and beautiful snowflakes fall when temperatures are close to freezing point, bringing 'wet' snow, and there is no wind. The largest snowflakes ever recorded fell in Fort Keogh, Montana, in January 1887, measuring, remarkably, 38cm across and 20cm thick.

THE MOUNTAIN RESCUER

IT WAS ABOUT SIX THIRTY WHEN I FLOPPED DOWN ON THE SOFA TO WATCH the telly with my two daughters. I can't have sat down for more than two minutes when the phone rang. 'That's strange,' I thought. 'There can't be an accident or an incident, can there? Surely not. No one goes climbing or caving today.' Since the Cave Rescue Organisation (CRO) was founded in 1935, they'd never had a callout on 25 December. There are always plenty on Boxing Day, but never on the main day. Not until 2006, that is – and quite a job it was going to be too. The policeman on the end of the line told me there'd been an accident in a set of caves at Easegill Caverns near Kirkby Lonsdale. A caver had fallen off a ledge and broken his pelvis. He was in agony. Leaving the injured man behind with the third man in the party, the other set off alone to raise the alarm.

The cavers had been doing a 'through trip', where you go in one entrance and come out another. It had taken the man four hours to find his exit before alerting us, which meant it would be almost half a day since the accident happened before we could get a rescue team and some doctors down to the injured man. I knew him – the caving and mountain-climbing community is pretty tight – and he certainly wasn't the type to whinge. He was a very experienced caver too, so I reckoned the accident had to be very serious.

I've been inside those caves many times and as soon as I heard that the injured man was deep inside them I realized it was going to be a major operation. The caves are huge and there are plenty of challenges, including drops to abseil down, narrow tunnels, and fast-moving streams.

Handily for me, the local rescue centre is right next door to my house in the Dales and immediately I started assembling the team as fast as I could. Deep-cave rescue involves a lot of manpower, partly because communication is difficult and you need a lot of bodies on the ground, and below it, to send messages back and forth. Obviously, mobiles don't work underground. Some of the people I contacted were unable to come straight away because, not being on call, they'd had a few drinks. Others were just sitting down to eat with their families when the phone rang. In the end, we had four rescue teams from across the north of England involved in order to locate all the skilled personnel we needed to carry out the job. There were 70 of us in all by the time the operation was fully under way.

The entrance to the caves is a 45-minute hike across moorland from the road, but we managed to get a reasonable body of men there fairly quickly given that it was Christmas Day. Luckily, another team of cavers, who had been alerted to the problem, had gone in before us with matting, blankets and insulation, which was great, because we knew the casualty was at least going to be warm. It wasn't an especially cold day – about seven degrees – but there are lots of draughts down there especially near the moving water, so it feels pretty chilly. Also, you get wet easily when caving, from sweating, crossing streams, squeezing against wet walls or crawling along the ground.

I was co-ordinating the operation from on top, and sent down two teams of men, including three doctors. The worst-case scenario was that the casualty would have to be carried out on a stretcher, which could take up to 12 hours. By their very nature, underground rescues generally take a long time in the most favourable circumstances, but this time it seemed to take forever for the first news of the man's condition and the progress of his rescue. There was a collective sigh of relief when word reached us on top that once the doctors had pumped him full of painkillers and put him in a splint, he was able to move.

When he finally emerged from underground at five thirty in the morning, fully 15 hours after injuring himself, there was a spontaneous round of applause. It's always a great moment, that. But we had another problem now. It's often the case that injured cavers or mountain climbers will be carried along by their adrenaline, but once they emerge above ground, or they feel they have done the hard part, their body closes down and they collapse. That's what happened to this guy. The cave entrance is in the middle of nowhere, so there was no chance of getting an ambulance up there. The RAF scrambled a Sea King helicopter for us, but due to the thick mist blanketing northern England it was delayed and couldn't get anywhere near the cave entrance. There was only one thing for it: we'd have to carry him on a stretcher to the road across the moorland. Luckily, the helicopter arrived just as the stretcher party reached the road. It only took a few minutes to carry him onboard and then it was straight off to hospital in Lancaster.

We were all pretty shattered by the time we had cleared up and left the site. I fell into bed at eight thirty in the morning on Boxing Day, and immediately descended into a very deep sleep. I was woken up by the sound of the phone in mid-afternoon. It was another callout. A family had got lost out in the Dales ...

TOM REDFERN, cave and mountain rescuer

Reindeer Sausages and Minced Coffins:

Christmas Food and Drink

Unfortunately, the Parisian 'blom budding', unless prepared by British hands, is generally a concoction of culinary atrocities, tasting, let us say, like saveloy soup and ginger bread porridge. In a few instances, the 'Angleesh blom budding' has been served at French tables in a soup tureen; and guests have been known to direct fearful and furtive glances towards it, just as an Englishman might regard with mingled feelings of surprise and suspicion a fricassee of frogs.

Daily Telegraph, **1886**

❄ ❄ ❄ ❄

A merry Christmas and a happy New Year,
Your pockets full of money and your cellar full of beer.

OLD SAYING

❄ ❄ ❄ ❄

Men may talk of country Christmases
Their thirty pound butter'd eggs,
Their pies of carps' tongues,
Their pheasants drench'd with ambergris:
The carcases of three fat wethers bruised for gravy;
To make sauce for a single peacock;
Yet their feasts were fasts
Compared with the city's.

PHILIP MASSINGER (1583–1640), English dramatist
The City Madam

To Roast a Turkey.

In very cold weather a turkey in its feathers will hang (in an airy larder) quite a fortnight with advantage; and, however fine a quality of bird it may be, unless sufficiently long kept, it will prove not worth the dressing, though it should always be perfectly sweet when prepared for table … Pluck, draw and singe it with exceeding care; wash and then dry it thoroughly with clean cloths, or merely wipe the outside well, without wetting it, and pour water plentifully through the inside. Fill the beast with forcemeat [a kind of stuffing], or with the finest sausage meat, highly seasoned with minced herbs, lemon-rind, mace and cayenne. Truss the bird firmly, lay it to a clear sound fire, baste it constantly and bountifully with butter and serve it when done with good brown gravy and well-made bread sauce. An entire chain of delicate fried sausages is still often placed in the dish, round a turkey, as a garnish … A turkey should be laid at first far from the fire, and drawn nearer when half done though never sufficiently so to scorch it; it should be as well roasted, for even the most inveterate advocates of under-dressed meat will seldom tolerate the taste or the sight of partially raw poultry.

ELIZA ACTON (1799–1859), English cook
Modern Cookery for Private Families, first published 1845

❋ ❋ ❋ ❋

Necessary Amount of Food

In estimating the amount of food to be taken by a healthy man during the twenty four hours [of Christmas Day], it has to be considered whether the person has work to perform, or if he will remain at rest; also if he has to work, whether his brain or muscles are to be employed. It has been proved by experience that the harder the work performed, the more food is required to replace the tissues worn away by the exertion. Food that contains much nitrogen is best suited for those who work by muscular exertion, while individuals who have to undergo much mental exertion, and thus wear away the tissues of the brain and nervous system, require principally food in which the phosphates are most abundant.

Cassell's Book of the Household, 1878

❋ ❋ ❋ ❋

IN 1819 COOKS IN DEVON PRODUCED A **CHRISTMAS pudding** weighing 900 pounds.

Christmas, n. A day set apart and consecrated to gluttony, drunkenness, maudlin sentiment, gift-taking, public dullness and domestic behaviour.

AMBROSE BIERCE (1842–1914), American writer
The Devil's Dictionary

❄ ❄ ❄ ❄

STILTON IS THE ONLY BRITISH CHEESE TO ENJOY LEGAL PROTECTION. Originally the cheese was known as Quenby, after a Midlands town of that name, but it gradually changed to Stilton in the early eighteenth century because the Bell Inn at Stilton sold it in such great quantities. Cooks, epicureans and scientists all seem to agree that the tradition of pouring wine into the bowl of a whole Stilton does neither the wine nor the cheese any favours. This apparently ridiculous custom arose out of a confusion about the manufacturing process.

❄ ❄ ❄ ❄

THE NAME 'TURKEY' IS THOUGHT TO HAVE BEEN GIVEN TO THE BIRD after a misunderstanding about its native habitat. The birds come from Mexico originally, but when they first arrived in England in the sixteenth century they were brought by sailors from the eastern Mediterranean known as 'Turkey merchants'. The English weren't the only people unsure about the strange-looking bird's origins. Most Europeans were under the impression it came from India, a confusion arising out of the newly discovered regions of the Caribbean and Central America, known as the Spanish Indies or the New Indies. *Indianischer Hahn*, for instance, is the old German for turkey while the Danes called it *kalkun* after the Indian port of Calcutta.

❄ ❄ ❄ ❄

THE FIRST WRITTEN REFERENCE IN BRITAIN TO 'TURKEY' COMES IN THE early 1500s, and by the late seventeenth century turkey farms were well established in East Anglia and Lincolnshire. As demand for the bird grew among Britain's expanding middle classes in the eighteenth century, great flocks of them set off in November and were **driven into London's markets** in time to be hung for the festive season.

Great Slaughter at Louth

On Friday week, Mr Valentine Fell, poulterer, of Louth, near Boston, assisted by forty-five persons, commenced his annual slaughtering of poultry for the Christmas market. No fewer than 4000 geese ... as well as 1500 ducks, turkeys and fowls, comprised the number to be slaughtered. They were all consigned to Leadenhall market, and were calculated to weigh upwards of thirty tons. Many of the geese were of remarkably large kind, and weighed from 16lb to 20lb.

Illustrated London News, **22 December 1849**

❋   ❋   ❋   ❋

At Christmas it was frequently the custom for each [peasant] tenant to give to the lord a hen (partly as payment for being allowed to keep poultry), or sometimes grain which was brewed into ale ... At Christmas also the lord was expected to give his tenants a meal, for example, bread, cheese, pottage and two dishes of meat. The tenant might be directed to bring his own plate, mug and napkin if he wished there to be a cloth on the table, and a faggot of brushwood to cook his food, unless he wished to have it raw. Sometimes the custom said explicitly that the lord had to give a Christmas meal because the tenant had given him the food. In at least one instance the value of the food to be provided by the lord was to be the same value as that given by the tenant. The role of the lord in this case appears to have been merely to organize the village Christmas dinner. The value of the dinner was not always so finely balanced as this however: sometimes the lord gained, sometimes the tenant. These customs were maintained for several centuries, lasting in some cases after the end of the manorial system when compulsory work had been commuted into the paying of rent.

P. W. HAMMOND

Food and Feast in Medieval England, 1993

❋   ❋   ❋   ❋

THE TURKEY WAS ORIGINALLY KNOWN IN PARTS OF FRANCE AS A *'JÉSUITE'*, after the Jesuit monastic order who brought the birds home from their **missionary endeavours** in Central America.

A noble dish is a turkey, roast or boiled. A Christmas dinner, with the middle classes of this empire, would scarcely be a Christmas dinner without its turkey; and we can hardly imagine an object of greater envy than is presented by a respected portly pater-familias carving, at the season devoted to good cheer and genial charity, his own fat turkey, and carving it well.

The only art consists, as in the carving of a goose, in getting from the breast as many fine slices as possible; and all must have remarked the very great difference in the large number of people whom a good carver will find slices for, and the comparatively few that a bad carver will succeed in serving. As we have stated in both the carving of a duck and goose, the carver should commence cutting slices close to the wing and then proceed upwards towards the ridge of the breastbone: this is not the usual plan, but, in practice, will be found the best.

The breast is the only part which is looked on as fine in a turkey, the legs being very seldom cut off and eaten at table: they are usually removed to the kitchen, where they are taken off, to appear only in a form which seems to have a special attraction at a bachelor's supper-table, we mean devilled: served in this way, they are especially liked and relished.

A boiled turkey is carved in the same manner as when roasted.

Mrs Beeton (1836–65), British cookery writer
Book of Household Management

... Meanwhile, it remains true that I shall eat a great deal of turkey this Christmas; and it is not in the least true (as the vegetarians say) that I shall do it because I do not realise what I am doing, or because I do what I know is wrong, or that I do it with shame or doubt or a fundamental unrest of conscience. In one sense I know quite well what I am doing; in another sense I know quite well that I know not what I do. Scrooge and the Cratchits and I are, as I have said, all in one boat; the turkey and I are, to say the most of it, ships that pass in the night, and greet each other in passing. I wish him well; but it is really practically impossible to discover whether I treat him well. I can avoid, and I do avoid with horror, all special and artificial tormenting of him, sticking pins in him for fun or sticking knives in him for scientific investigation. But whether by feeding him slowly and killing him quickly for the

needs of my brethren, I have improved in his own solemn eyes his own strange and separate destiny, whether I have made him in the sight of God a slave or a martyr, or one whom the gods love and who die young — that is far more removed from my possibilities of knowledge than the most abstruse intricacies of mysticism or theology. A turkey is more occult and awful than all the angels and archangels in so far as God has partly revealed to us an angelic world, he has partly told us what an angel means. But God has never told us what a turkey means. And if you go and stare at a live turkey for an hour or two, you will find by the end of it that the enigma has rather increased than diminished.

G. K. CHESTERTON (1874–1936), English writer
All Things Considered: Christmas

❋ ❋ ❋ ❋

Two centuries ago every well-to-do family made a Christmas pie or shred pie: 'a most learned mixture of neats' tongues, chickens, eggs, sugar, raisins etc ...' They ought to be confined to the season of Christmas. No modern receipts [recipes] are similar and the less meat they contain the better.

Cassell's Book of the Household, 1878

❋ ❋ ❋ ❋

A CHRISTMAS PUDDING IN THE MIDDLE AGES TOOK THE FORM OF spicy porridge known as 'frumenty'. The dish was considered a tremendous treat, even by over-indulged royals and noblemen, already at bursting point after a week of feasting on peacocks, oxen, swans, boars and small peasants. It consisted mainly of **cracked wheat boiled in animal stock** and mixed with egg yolks and threads of the highly prized spice saffron. Recipes differed from region to region and household to household but most came to include sweeter spices like cinnamon and nutmeg, as well as currants and other dried fruit. The mixture was left to set before being served, often as an accompaniment to meat dishes.

SPROUTS USED TO BE HIGHLY CHERISHED BY BRITONS BECAUSE THEY are one of the few fresh vegetables available in the winter months. They are also highly nutritious. Ounce for ounce, they have three times the level of vitamin C of an orange, and just five of them contain the full amount an adult requires in a day. Sprouts are also a good source of vitamin D and folic acid during pregnancy, and have specific health-promoting compounds called glucosinolates that may help to prevent cancer. In recent times, they have been shunted aside on supermarket shelves by their trendier, more exotic cousins from abroad. Consider it an act of patriotism then, as well as kindness towards the environment, the next time you go shopping and eschew the air-delivered curly kale from China to choose instead some home-grown Brussels.

❊   ❊   ❊   ❊

A dog isn't just for Christmas.
It's jolly nice cold on Boxing Day too.
ENGLISH SAYING

❊   ❊   ❊   ❊

So coming to Calas [Calais] the next day it was Christmas Day and the first
Christmas Day ever I had out of England, but not the last by a great many. We
had but small Christmas cheer, not having Christmas pie or roast beef, or plum
podich and suchlike, I remember that the poorest people in England would have a
bit of something that was good on such a day, and that many beggars would fare
much better than we did: for we had nothing but a little bit of Irish beef for four
men, which had lain in pickle two or three years and was rusty as the devil, with
a little stinking oil or butter, which was all colours of the rainbow, many men in
England greasing their cartwheels with better: and also we had not two or three
days to play in and go where we would, as the worst servants had in England, but
as soon as we had ate our large dinner, which was done in three or four mouthfuls,
we must work all the day after, and maybe a great part of the night.

SEAMAN JOHN BARLOW
Journal, Christmas 1661

❊   ❊   ❊   ❊

A WARNING TO VIRGIN CHRISTMAS **duck-eaters**: the bones of a duck are much heavier than those of a turkey or chicken, so you need a bigger bird to get the same amount of meat.

SALES OF **GOOSE FAT** HAVE ROCKETED IN RECENT YEARS AFTER SEVERAL television chefs championed this once-common food item. Used in the past as a hand cream and a treatment for chilblains, the fat is superb for frying eggs and roasting potatoes, owing to the very high temperatures it can reach without burning.

CHRISTMAS LUNCH TIPS

If you've drawn the short straw and have been elected to remove the innards of your fresh turkey, be careful with its gall bladder, that nasty-looking little green sack attached to the liver. If it bursts, the bile will seep into the meat and give it a very unhealthy appearance.

Panfry the liver and eat it on toast, like hot pâté.

Get rid of feathery tufts by passing the bird over an open flame.

Stuffing turkey may be traditional but it slows up the cooking time, and makes the bird more susceptible to drying out. If you do stuff it, you will have to baste the bird at regular intervals to keep the moisture in. Better, then, to make stuffing separately and put onions and lemon halves in the cavity and pour some water into the bottom of the foil. This will improve the flavour and keep it moist.

For the best flavour and texture, cook the turkey upside down so that all juices run into the white meat. It looks weird, but then turkeys don't exactly look handsome or 'normal' at the best of times, alive or dead.

It's easier to carve a turkey if you take its legs off first.

If your gravy is too thin, just make a quick paste of butter and flour and stir it in.

To remove the excess fat from gravy, let it cool a little and then drop in a couple of ice cubes. The fat will congeal more quickly, allowing you to lift it out more easily.

You can extract the natural sweetness of carrots, onions and parsnips by adding a sprinkle of sugar while they cook. A big nob of butter will give them a fine glaze.

Christmas Lunch Short Cuts

★ Stick chipolatas on a skewer so that you can turn them all at once, rather than one by one while you curse the day Christmas ever came into existence.

★ For a quick alternative to roast or boiled root vegetables, make them into a gratin by slicing them thinly and covering each layer with a mixture of milk, cream, nutmeg and whole grain mustard, adding slices of garlic and onions to concentrate the flavour.

★ Buy supermarket mincemeat for the Christmas pudding or mince pies and throw in a few of your own ingredients (nuts, dried fruit) and brandy to give it a more home-made feel.

★ It will be several days before you can get your hands on the turkey bones to make a stock as you work your way through the carcass of meat. But you can make an instant stock as follows: put the turkey giblets into a bowl with an onion, a carrot, water and seasoning and then blast in the microwave until it's done (roughly 10 to 15 minutes).

★ Improve cheap crackers by slipping in through the ends extra gifts (such as good chocolates, 10 Rothmans, etc.).

Typical Swedish Smörgåsbord on Christmas Day

CHRISTMAS HAM, PORK SAUSAGE, HERRING SALAD, PICKLED HERRING, home-made liver pâté, egg and anchovy mix (*gubbröra*), flavoured rye bread (*vörtbröd*), potatoes and a special fish dish called *lutfisk*. The ham is boiled, then basted with a mixture of egg, breadcrumbs and mustard before it is grilled for a glazed effect. *Lutfisk* is dried ling soaked in water and lye so that it swells before it is cooked.

❄ ❄ ❄ ❄

Christmas is a season of such infinite labour, as well as expense in the shopping and present-making line, that almost every woman I know is good for nothing in purse and person for a month afterwards, done up physically, and broken down financially.

FANNY KEMBLE (1809–93), British actress and author

Potages
Consommé à la Monaco. Du Berry.

Poissons
Filet de Sole à la Vassant.
Eperlans frits, sauce Verneuil.

Entrée
Côtelettes de Volaille à la York.

Relevés
Dinde à la Chipolata.
Roast Beef. Chine of Pork.

Entremêts
Asperges, sauce Hollandaise.
Mince Pies. Plum Pudding.
Gelée d'Orange à l'Anglaise.

Buffet
Baron of Beef.
Boar's Head.
Game Pie.
Woodcock Pie.
Brawn.
Roast Fowl.
Tongue.

Queen Victoria's Christmas Dinner at Windsor in 1899

Christmas Plum Pudding

The plum pudding is a national dish, and is despised by foreign nations because they never can make it fit to eat. In almost every family there is a recipe for it, which has been handed down from mother to daughter through two or three generations, and which never has been and never will be equalled, much less surpassed, by any other ... It is usual, before sending it to the table, to make a little hole in the top and fill it with brandy, then light it, and serve it in a blaze. In olden time a sprig of arbutus, with a red berry on it, was stuck in the middle, and a twig of variegated holly, with berries, placed on each side. This was done to keep away witches ... If well made, Christmas plum pudding will be good for twelve months.

Cassell's Dictionary of Cookery, 1875

❄ ❄ ❄ ❄

The greatest of the feasts celebrated was Christmas. This, of course, covered twelve days, but unlike the modern Christmas the celebrations did not begin until Christmas Day itself. Advent was mostly a time of fasting, and as Advent only ended after mass on Christmas Day, the festivities could not begin before then ...

Christmas, then as now, had a variety of dishes associated with it. The first was the boar's head, which formed the centrepiece of the Christmas Day meal. It was garnished with rosemary and bay and evidently was presented to the diners with some style, as told by the many boar's head carols which still exist ... Thomas Tusser in Five Hundred Points of Good Husbandry *suggests a number of dishes that, lower down society, the housewife should provide for her guests at Christmas. He mentions mutton, pork, veal souse (pickled pig's feet and ears), brawn, cheese and apples, although none of these items was connected especially with Christmas; they were all associated with feasting generally. He also talks of serving turkey, but only as a part of a list of other luxurious items that the housewife should provide. It does not seem to be the centrepiece in the way that the boar's head was in grander circles.*

ALISON SIM
Food and Feast in Tudor England, 1997

LOVERS OF BRUSSELS SPROUTS SAY THE REASON WHY THE REST OF US loathe them is down to the fact that we don't know how to cook them properly. Invariably they are overdone, which removes the sweetness, but cooked properly, this much-libelled vegetable possesses a delicate flavour. Overcooking releases sulphur compounds in the sprouts, creating the vegetable's characteristic farty aroma, or 'a powerful smell of drains' as the Victorians euphemistically put it. Steaming, rather than boiling them, helps to preserve their sweetness. Some claim sprouts are better in late winter after they have enjoyed the benefit of a **few sharp frosts**.

Not drunk is he who from the floor
Can rise alone and still drink more
But drunk is he who prostrate lies,
Without the power to drink and rise.

THOMAS LOVE PEACOCK (1785–1866)
The Misfortunes of Elphin, 1829

✳ ✳ ✳ ✳

THE FIRST WRITTEN REFERENCE TO SPROUTS IS FOUND IN 1587, AND they became known as Brussels sprouts because of their **great popularity in Belgium**.

✳ ✳ ✳ ✳

CUTTING A CROSS ON THE BASE OF A SPROUT IS AN OLD ENGLISH custom performed partly out of a belief that the inside will then cook at the same rate as the outside, but also out of the superstition that it will **keep out the devil**. (Our ancestors were quick to accuse vegetables of consorting with Satan. Broad beans, in particular, came under heavy suspicion for many centuries, probably as a result of the vegetables' tendency to cause unsettled sleep if eaten late in the evening.) Today, most cooks contest that 'crossing' lets the flavour escape and should thus be avoided. Ramming home their point, 'anti-crossers' will also tell you that the practice loosens the leaves and may even lead to the total disintegration of the vegetable.

A TURTLE ENJOYING A SPECIAL CHRISTMAS meal of Brussels sprouts triggered a Boxing Day emergency in 2006 when it set off an alarm at an aquatic centre in Weymouth – by **passing wind**. The fart bubbles rose to the surface of the turtle's water tank where they popped and splashed water on to an alarm sensor, bringing the local firecrews haring to the scene in a blare of sirens and flashing blue lights.

❄ ❄ ❄ ❄

LATE DECEMBER WAS A LOGICAL TIME OF YEAR FOR OUR ANCESTORS TO have a feast, being the season when food harvested in the autumn needed finishing up before it succumbed to decay, and animals that struggle for food in winter were slaughtered. It was also the time when beers and wines, made in the autumn, were **mature enough to drink**. Pigs were often killed at the year's end because they had scoffed most of the beechnuts and acorns that autumn had strewn for them over the woodland floor. For centuries pigs and boars formed the focus of the Christmas feast in northern European cultures. The little sausages, bacon rolls and joints of ham we eat with our turkey today are a leftover of that long-standing tradition.

ON WITH THE PLAY!

*CROMWELL IS DEAD
LONG LIVE CHRISTMAS!*

MINCE PIES WERE SOMETIMES KNOWN AS 'COFFINS' IN SOME PARTS OF England because they were once rectangular in shape. Sometimes they were made to look like **a manger with a pastry baby stuck on top**. It was no surprise that the Puritans, great despisers of frivolity and humour, condemned the crib-shaped pastries as popish works of the devil. When Christmas re-emerged with the restoration of the monarchy in the 1660s, it was different from what it used to be in its small details as well as its general atmosphere. Overall, the celebrations were more subdued than they had been in the Middle Ages. The mince pie was not immune from the changes: it had become round, with no baby on top.

Superlative Mincemeat

Take four large lemons with their weight of golden pippins pared and cored, of jar-raisins, candied citron and orange rind; and the finest suet, and a fourth part of sugar.

Boil the lemons tender, chop them small, but be careful just to extract the pips. Add them to the other ingredients after all have been prepared with great nicety, and mix the whole well with from three to four glasses of brandy, a pinch of salt, some nutmeg and mace and ginger (two whole nutmegs going to 10lb mincemeat plus one large teaspoon of pounded mace and rather more of ginger).

ELIZA ACTON
Modern Cookery for Private Families, 1845

❊ ❊ ❊ ❊

UNTIL THE MID-NINETEENTH CENTURY WHEN TURKEY BECAME THE centrepiece of the Christmas Day feast, there was something of a **north–south divide** over the main meal. In the north they tended to eat roast beef, and in the south they ate goose.

❊ ❊ ❊ ❊

ONE OF THE REASONS WHY THE TURKEY SUPPLANTED THE GOOSE AS the main Christmas dish was its great size. Middle-class families had grown larger in Victorian times, and wider family gatherings were made possible by improved transport. One large turkey was capable of feeding a dozen or more diners. Owing to the bird's breeding habits, geese were also tougher and less appetizing than the succulent and novel turkey. Once, most geese were born in the spring and eaten young in the late summer or early autumn after they had been fattened in the freshly harvested cornfields. This was also the time of year when, happily, apples and chestnuts — fine accompaniments to goose — were in season. By Christmas, though, the goose had become a **tough old bird**, especially the ones who had spent weeks walking from East Anglia to their festive slaughter in London. Today, farmers are able to engineer breeding times so that the birds that appear at Christmas are much younger and tastier. The principle still holds good that the smaller the bird, the younger and more tender it will be.

HUGE SAVOURY PIES, STUFFED WITH EVERY MANNER OF BEAST AND bird, used to be a commonplace sight in British households. It's strange that they have gone out of fashion, or at best have been reduced to pathetic little parcels. One of the savoury pie's great virtues is that it will keep for some time when refrigerated. It is delicious eaten cold with pickles and a salad. Below is a recipe for a truly sumptuous Yorkshire Christmas pie from the great Charles Elme Francatelli, an Anglo-Italian cook who rose from humble origins to become Queen Victoria's chef. It is taken from his excellent book *A Modern Cook*, published in 1845. In 1861, he produced another classic, *A Plain Cookery Book for the Working Classes*, in which, like Jamie Oliver today, he sought to persuade ordinary people of the benefits of wholesome, healthy cooking.

First, bone a turkey, a goose, a brace of young pheasants, four partridges, four woodcocks, a dozen snipes, four grouse, and four widgeons; then boil and trim a small York ham and two tongues. Season and garnish the inside of the fore-named game and poultry with long fillets of fat bacon and tongue, and French truffles; each must be carefully sewn up with a needle and small twine, so as to prevent the force-meat from escaping while they are being baked. When the whole of these are ready, line two round or oval braizing-pans with thin layers of fat bacon, and after the birds have been arranged therein in neat order, and covered in with layers of bacon and buttered paper, put the lids on, and set them in the oven to bake rather slowly, for about four hours: then withdraw them, and allow them to cool.

While the foregoing is in progress, prepare some highly-seasoned aspic-jelly with the carcasses of the game and poultry, to which add six calves' feet, and the usual complement of vegetables, &c., and when done, let it be clarified: one-half should be reduced previously to its being poured into the pie when it is baked.

Make about sixteen pounds of hot-water-paste, and use it to raise a pie of sufficient dimensions to admit of its holding the game and poultry prepared for the purpose ... The inside of the pie must first be lined with thin layers of fat bacon, over which spread a coating of well-seasoned force-meat of fat; the birds should then be placed in the following order: First, put the goose at the bottom with some of the small birds

round it, filling up the cavities with some of the force-meat; then, put the turkey and the pheasants with thick slices of the boiled ham between them, reserving the woodcocks and widgeons, that these may be placed on the top: fill the cavities with force-meat and truffles, and cover the whole with thin layers of fat bacon, run a little plain melted butter over the surface, cover the pie in the usual manner, and ornament it with a bold design. The pie must now be baked, for about six hours, in an oven moderately heated, and when taken out, and after the reduced aspic above alluded to has been poured into it, stop the hole up with a small piece of paste, and set it aside in the larder to become cold.

NOTE: The quantity of game, &c., recommended to be used in the preparation of the foregoing pie may appear extravagant enough, but it is to be remembered that these very large pies are mostly in request at Christmas time. Their substantial aspect renders them worthy of appearing on the side-table of those wealthy epicures who are wont to keep up the good old English style, at this season of hospitality and good cheer.

❋ ❋ ❋ ❋

FROM THE MID-1850S, WHILE MORE AND MORE WELL-TO-DO Victorians began to treat the Christmas period as a time of holiday, many **shopkeepers and tradesmen continued to work**. As a gesture of seasonal goodwill, the local baker, who had to keep his fires burning continuously, was often in the habit of letting the poor people in his neighbourhood cook their Christmas geese in his huge ovens.

❋ ❋ ❋ ❋

There never was such a goose. Bob said he didn't believe there ever was such a goose cooked. Its tenderness and flavour, size and cheapness, were the themes of universal admiration. Eked out by apple-sauce and mashed potatoes, it was a sufficient dinner for the whole family; indeed, as Mrs Cratchit said with great delight (surveying one small atom of a bone upon the dish), they hadn't ate it all at last! Yet every one had had enough, and the youngest Cratchits in particular, were steeped in sage and onion to the eyebrows!

CHARLES DICKENS
A Christmas Carol, 1843

AS IF SHE DIDN'T HAVE ENOUGH ON HER PLATE ALREADY, NIGELLA Lawson has taken time to come up with a brilliant plan to increase the **juiciness** of Britain's 10 million Christmas turkeys. All you need is a large bucket, or a small tub, lots of water, a cupboard full of spices and other goodies — and a memo stuck on the fridge to remind you to prepare it all 48 hours before you plan to put the turkey in the oven. In her book *Feast*, Nigella produces a list of perfect ingredients to add to the water, but I'm sure it wouldn't be a disaster if you were missing a few of them or opted to substitute some with similar alternatives. Once you have submerged the turkey, leave it outside, or somewhere cold, and make sure you cover it with something heavy — unless you want every fox in the neighbourhood dropping by for a snack. Take it out an hour before cooking, and dry it. Nigella suggests the following: for 6 litres of water, add 250g salt, 3 tbsp peppercorns, a bouquet garni, 2 tbsp white mustard seeds, 200g caster sugar, 2 peeled and quartered onions, a slice of ginger, 1 cinnamon stick, 1 tbsp caraway seeds, 4 cloves, 2 tbsp allspice berries, 4 star anise, 1 orange, 4 tbsp maple syrup, 4 tbsp runny honey and some parsley stalks.

IT WAS A VICTORIAN SUPERSTITION THAT EVERY MEMBER OF THE HOUSE must **stir the Christmas pudding mix** in a particular direction, or bring bad luck upon them all — though which direction they meant seems to have been a moot point. Some said it was east to west, in honour of the three wise men coming from the Orient, while others said clockwise, and still others right to left. (Historians can only guess whether General Gordon of Khartoum had stirred his Christmas pudding the wrong way.) On ships, the rules of the superstition were more straightforward: so long as the captain gave it a stir, the gods would look favourably on the vessel.

A great deal of steam! The pudding was out of the copper. A smell like a washing-day! That was the cloth! A smell like an eating-house and a pastry cook's next door to each other, with a laundress's next door to that! That was the pudding. In half a minute, Mrs Cratchit entered — flushed, but smiling proudly — with the pudding, like a speckled cannon-ball, so hard and firm, blazing in half-a-quartern of ignited brandy, and bedight with Christmas holly stuck into the top. Oh, a wonderful pudding. Bob Cratchit said, and calmly too, that he regarded it as the greatest success achieved by Mrs Cratchit since their marriage. Mrs Cratchit said that now the weight was off her mind, she would confess she had had her doubts about the quantity of flour.

CHARLES DICKENS
A Christmas Carol, 1843

DRUNK CHRISTMAS CAKE

1 pint water
1 mug sugar
4 large eggs
2 cups dried fruit
1 tsp salt
1 cup demerara sugar
3 cups nuts
2 tbsp lemon juice
1 orange rind
1 very large bottle of whisky

Try the whisky to check for good quality. Find a large bowl. Check the whisky again to make sure it hasn't gone off in the meantime. Just to be extra sure, pour a proper glass of it and drink. Repeat until absolutely certain. Turn on the food professor, and beat up the butter in the large bowl. Add sugar and beat the buffer again. Check the whisky is still room temperature. Turn up the volume on the processor. Lob the five beggs into the bowl and chuck in the fup of cried druit. Mix on the whizzy turner thing. If the fired druit gets stuck in the food professor's blades, lisdodge the gunk. Sample the whisky to check no one has sneaked in and diluted it. Next, the salt. Or whatever. Make sure whisky is still smooth to the tongue. Now shit the lemon juice and strain your nuts. Add one table of lemon. Do the sugar or something. Whatever's to hand. Wash down the oven. Turn the cake tin to 450 degrees. Burn off the food professor. Drop the bowl on the floor, go to bed taking care to bring whisky bottle with you in case it falls into wrong hands. Lie down and enjoy a warm glow of satisfaction at a job well done.

*Ha più da fare che
i forni di Natale in
Inghilterra.*

('He has more to do than the ovens
in England at Christmas.')

ITALIAN PROVERB

❋ ❋ ❋ ❋

*To make up for the shortage of shell
eggs, there will be a double ration
of dried eggs. Between now and
Christmas there will be an acute
shortage of fruit. There are practically
no apples on the market, and it is
doubtful if many children will get
oranges. The sale of nuts is practically
non-existent. For those who may
be eating in restaurants during
Christmas there should
be plenty of
fish ... British
troops on
duty in Home
Commands will have
an egg with their bacon for
breakfast; roast pork or poultry,
potatoes, sprouts and Christmas
pudding for dinner; while
teatime will bring cake and
mince pies.*

News of the World,
19 December 1943

❋ ❋ ❋ ❋

REINDEER MEAT
is very popular in the
Scandinavian countries
and among other people living
close to the Arctic Circle. The
Lapps serve **smoked roast**
reindeer in thin slices and in
sandwiches. They also serve it
sautéed as a main dish. The
meat has a mild gamy flavour
and is packed with goodness,
partly because of the good food
the animal eats, including
'reindeer moss', which is packed
with vitamin C. Reindeer
meatballs are sold in cans in
Alaska, and reindeer sausages
are a common sight in local
stores.

❋ ❋ ❋ ❋

*A man might then behold
At Christmas, in each hall
Good fires to curb the cold,
And meat for great and
small.
The neighbours
were friendly bidden,
And all had
welcome true,
The poor from
the gates were not
chidden,
When this old cap
was new.*

OLD ENGLISH SONG

❋ ❋ ❋ ❋

*Our [Christmas Day] breakfast
consisted of what the Squire
denominated true old English
fare. He indulged in some bitter
lamentations over modern breakfasts
of tea-and-toast, which he censured*

as among the causes of modern effeminacy and weak nerves, and the decline of old English heartiness; and though he admitted them to his table to suit the palates of his guests, yet there was a brave display of cold meats, wine and ale, on the sideboard.

WASHINGTON IRVING
The Sketch Book, 1819–20

IN A LETTER OF 1784 TO HIS daughter, Benjamin Franklin, one of the Founding Fathers of the United States of America, lamented that the turkey had not been chosen ahead of the eagle as the country's official bird. The following is an excerpt from the letter:

For my own part I wish the Bald Eagle had not been chosen the Representative of our Country. He is a Bird of bad moral Character. He does not get his Living honestly. You may have seen him perched on some dead Tree near the River, where, too lazy to fish for himself, he watches the Labour of the Fishing Hawk; and when that diligent Bird has at length taken a Fish, and is bearing it to his Nest for the Support of his Mate and young Ones, the Bald Eagle pursues him and takes it from him.

With all this Injustice, he is never in good Case but like those among Men who live by Sharping & Robbing he is generally poor and often very lousy. Besides he is a rank Coward: The little King Bird not bigger than a Sparrow attacks him boldly and drives him out of the District. He is therefore by no means a proper Emblem for the brave and honest Cincinnati of America who have driven all the King birds from our Country …

I am on this account not displeased that the Figure is not known as a Bald Eagle, but looks more like a Turkey. For in Truth the Turkey is in Comparison a much more respectable Bird, and withal a true original Native of America … He is besides, though a little vain and silly, a Bird of Courage, and would not hesitate to attack a Grenadier of the British Guards who should presume to invade his Farm Yard with a red Coat on.

Cheap Christmas Pudding

Now that eggs are 2d. each and sultana raisins 1s. a pound, a really cheap Christmas pudding would be a positive boon to many. The following recipe will not be found in any cookery book, as it is the result of some experiments I made with dates a few weeks ago. Dates are now retailed at 2d. a pound and enable us to make a rich, nourishing, and wholesome pudding, closely resembling Christmas pudding in appearance and flavour, sufficient for six persons, at a cost of 4d. Take a quarter of a pound each of suet, flour, and brown sugar (Porto Rico), one pound of dates, and a quarter of a grated nutmeg. Chop the suet finely, stone and cut up the dates, mix all the ingredients well together, moistening with as little water as possible; boil the whole in a buttered basin for four hours.

The Times, 24 December 1890

* * * *

Eggnog

To make a gallon of this eggnog will require a pound and a quarter of pulverized sugar, twelve fresh eggs, a quart of cognac, half a pint of champagne, two quarts of fresh milk, one quart of rich cream, and about a tablespoonful of powdered nutmeg. Mix these ingredients thoroughly, then incorporate with them the yolks of the dozen eggs that have been beaten to a froth. Stir persistently and steadily until the blend is perfect; pour the result into the well chilled punch bowl, and if you can procure some very old rum, add about three tablespoonfuls. Beat the white of the twelve eggs until very stiff, place this meringue on top of the eggnog, and you may feel reasonably assured that your guests will have no cause to complain about your mode of entertainment.

New York Times, 15 December 1907

* * * *

RESEARCHERS IN THE NETHERLANDS RECENTLY COMPLETED A LONG investigation into the effect of a diet high in Brussels sprouts on DNA damage. Of 10 healthy male volunteers, five ate a diet that included about 10 ounces of sprouts a day, while the other five ate a diet free of them and all other cruciferous vegetables. After three weeks, the sprout group showed a **28 per cent decrease** in measured DNA damage. The finding was considered important because scientists believe that any reduction in DNA damage could mean a reduction in the risk of inherited forms of cancer.

THE AUSTRALIAN *WOMAN'S MIRROR*, A MAGAZINE PUBLISHED between 1924 and 1961, produced a famous recipe in 1927 called 'Empire Christmas Pudding', encouraging its readers to show their loyalty to the British Crown. All of its ingredients were sourced from colonies and dominions of the British Empire:

5lb. sultanas (**Australia**)
5lb. currants (**Australia**)
5lb. stoned raisins (**South Africa**)
1½lb. minced apple (**Canada**)
5lb. breadcrumbs (**United Kingdom**)
5lb. beef suet (**New Zealand**)
2lb. cut candied peel (**South Africa**)
2½lb. flour (**United Kingdom**)
20 eggs (**Irish Free State**)
2½lb. Demerara sugar (**West Indies**)
2oz. ground cinnamon (**Ceylon**)
1½oz. ground cloves (**Zanzibar**)
1½oz. ground nutmegs (**Straits Settlements**)
1 teaspoonful pudding spice (**India**)
2 gills rum (**Jamaica**)
1 gill brandy (**Cyprus**)
2 quarts old beer (**England**)

Christmas Feast Recipes

STILTON AND CELERIAC SOUP

2 medium onions, chopped ✱ 2 medium potatoes, chopped
✱ 1 large celeriac, peeled and diced ✱ 250ml dry cider
✱ 1 litre chicken or vegetable stock ✱ 100ml double cream
✱ 400g Stilton, crumbled

Gently fry the onion, potato and celeriac until they soften, add
the cider and stock and simmer for 20 minutes or so. Let it cool a
little, then liquidize. Return the liquid to the pan, add the Stilton
and cream and reheat, stirring gently. Crumble some Stilton on top
before serving.

PERFECT ROAST POTATOES

Cut floury potatoes, such as Maris Piper or King Edward, to the size
required and parboil for about five minutes, then drain and shake
them around the pan to roughen the surfaces.
Goose fat is superb for roasting but olive oil
will do fine. In a (hot) pre-heated oven, place
a roasting tin containing a generous quantity
of fat or oil. When it starts to smoke, take the
tin out and pour in the potatoes, basting them
all over before returning them to the oven. Let
them cook for about an hour, turning them
from time to time to ensure all sides are
done equally.

ROAST GOOSE

Roasting a goose is pretty straightforward
as the bird bastes itself. It's best to
drain much of the fat from the
goose at the outset, otherwise it will
be too greasy for all except people
who live in caves. To degrease it,
prick dozens of holes all over the
bird, and place it on a slatted

tray over a roasting tin in an oven pre-heated to 180°C/ 350°F/Gas Mark 4. Leave for roughly an hour. Make sure the temperature isn't too high at any point during the roasting or the skin will blister and burn. Take the goose out and pat it all over with kitchen towel, inside as well, to soak up as much grease as possible. Add the stuffing of your choice (many chefs recommend a sweeter stuffing with goose, perhaps one made with cranberries and other dried fruit). Put it back in the oven in a roasting pan and let it cook for 25 minutes per pound, minus the hour it has already had to degrease it. Rebaste every half-hour using its own considerable juices.

STIR-FRIED SPICY RED CABBAGE WITH APPLES

If you're short of time – or it's Boxing Day and you've had enough of the stove – a quick alternative to traditional braised red cabbage is to stir-fry it. One of the great features of red cabbage is that, unlike most vegetables, it is better the day after it's cooked.

50g butter ✳ 2 tbsp oil ✳ 1 large onion, chopped ✳ 2 sweet apples, cored and chopped ✳ 3 garlic cloves, chopped ✳ 500g red cabbage ✳ Generous pinches of cinnamon, nutmeg and cloves ✳ Seasoning to taste ✳ 1 tbsp brown sugar ✳ 1 tbsp red wine vinegar

Melt the butter and oil in a large heavy frying pan or a wok with a heavy base. Soften the onion for a couple of minutes, then add the apple and garlic and cook for another two minutes. Turn up the heat and add the cabbage, stirring and turning it constantly with a wooden spoon as it fries. After a few minutes add the spices and seasoning; reduce the heat and leave it for 5 or 10 minutes, giving it the odd stir. When it's virtually done, turn the heat up again before stirring in the sugar and vinegar. Stir everything thoroughly, then serve.

CHESTNUT AND CRANBERRY STUFFING

300g chestnuts ✳ 250g cranberries, dried or fresh ✳ 500g sausage
meat ✳ Zest of one orange ✳ Pinch of nutmeg and cinnamon

If you use fresh chestnuts, make a slight incision in their shells
before placing them in a hot oven. When the shells open up, peel
them off together with the first layer of the skin. Wash the chestnuts
and chop them very coarsely before combining with the sausage
meat, orange zest, cranberries, spices and salt and pepper. Take all
the ingredients and knead into a big gooey mess before plunging it
all into the cavity of your bird.

CRANBERRY, PORT AND ORANGE SAUCE

1 large orange ✳ 150g caster sugar ✳ 100ml port ✳ 300g cranberries,
fresh or frozen ✳ 1 medium apple, finely chopped

Grate orange zest and squeeze the juice. Dissolve the sugar in a pan
with the juice and all but a drop of the port. Add the cranberries, apple
and orange rind and cook for about 10 minutes until the mixture has
softened and the juice has become stickier. Add the last dash of port.

PROPER BRUSSELS SPROUTS

Steam the sprouts for seven to eight minutes, then toss them in
butter, fresh herbs, chopped garlic, salt and pepper. They are even
better if you add some shallots and bacon that you've cooked in a
neighbouring frying pan.

MULLED CIDER MAKES A GOOD ALTERNATIVE TO mulled wine, especially if served after Christmas either before or with a rough-and-ready meal of leftover meats, vegetables and pickles.

MULLED CIDER

7 medium apples ✳ 12 whole cloves ✳ 5 pints good-quality cider ✳ 3 cinnamon sticks ✳ 1 orange ✳ 200g sugar ✳ ½ teaspoon ground ginger ✳ ½ teaspoon ground nutmeg

Spike six apples with cloves and bake. When they are soft, place in a large saucepan over medium heat and add the cider and all other ingredients. Bring to the boil then reduce to simmer for 30 minutes or so. Strain the mixture and serve with slices of apple and orange.

A POINSETTIA IS A FINE COCKTAIL TO SERVE AT CHRISTMAS TIME. IT'S so easy to prepare that even an idiot or a politician can make one. You wouldn't want more than a couple of them, though, unless you want to end up face down in the sprouts. The cocktail is a simple mixture of dry sparkling white wine, vodka or Cointreau and cranberry juice. Mix to taste and preferred strength.

✺ Christmas Leftover Recipes ✺

Roasted turkey, like chicken, is more flavoursome when reheated a day or two later. Below are some simple suggestions for using up what remains of your turkey and other Christmas foods. All the recipes are for four servings, unless otherwise stated.

SIMPLE CORONATION TURKEY

This is a very quick and easy dish, which can be used to fill sandwiches or baked potatoes, or served as it comes with salads and cold meats. Simply take a mixing bowl, add the following and stir it around until it is well combined: chopped turkey, mayonnaise, curry powder, raisins or sultanas, crumbled walnuts or almonds, chopped dried apricots, some honey or apricot jam or mango chutney.

LIARS' HOME-MADE CHRISTMAS PUDDING ICE CREAM

If you happen to have an ice-cream machine as well as a couple of hours to spare during your hectic Christmas schedule, then you could produce your own home-made Christmas pudding ice cream and wow your friends and relatives. Alternatively, you can save yourself all the bother, cheat shamelessly and still take all the glory by lying through your teeth about the great lengths you went to in its preparation. Half an hour or so before pudding, slip into the kitchen and take a tub of good quality vanilla ice cream (i.e. it doesn't taste too artificial) out of the freezer and leave it somewhere discreet so it can start to thaw. When it is soft enough, scoop it into a bowl, crumble and stir in the leftover Christmas pudding and then, to a standing ovation and frenzy of backslapping, serve up in individual bowls to your highly impressed guests. If the applause becomes prolonged and embarrassing, hold up your hand like a traffic policeman and say: 'Please, please. It was nothing. HONESTLY.' **A word of warning: don't re-freeze the ice cream if it has melted, unless you want to spend New Year's Eve on the loo.**

STILTON AND TURKEY SOUP

Serves 6 to 8.

1.5 litres stock made from the turkey bones ✳ 2 tbsp vegetable or olive oil ✳ 200g celery ✳ 100g carrots ✳ 150g onions ✳ 150g leeks ✳ 150g potato ✳ 1 tbsp plain flour ✳ 250g Stilton ✳ 250ml single cream

Coarsely chop all the vegetables. Heat the oil in a pan and cook the vegetables over a low heat for 10 to 15 minutes until soft. Stir in the flour, slowly add the stock and let it all simmer for about 40 minutes. Add the cream and Stilton and stir until the cheese melts. Season to taste. For a smoother finish, blend the soup in a food processor, but serve it as it comes if you want to keep it chunky and 'rustic'.

MASHED POTATO WITH STILTON AND TOASTED WALNUTS

150g Stilton ✳ 4 large potatoes ✳ 75g chopped walnuts ✳ ¾ cup milk ✳ Salt, pepper and nutmeg

Make the mashed potato as normal, stirring in the milk and making sure there are no lumps. Toast the walnuts. Mix in the nuts, crumble in the Stilton and season to taste with salt, pepper and nutmeg.

TURKEY HASH

1 medium onion (chopped) ✳ 1 red pepper (deseeded and chopped) ✳ 2 waxy potatoes (chopped) ✳ olive oil ✳ 300g chopped turkey ✳ chopped sage (preferably fresh) ✳ 6 eggs ✳ 8 rashers rindless bacon ✳ 4 tablespoons crème fraîche

Cook the onion, red pepper and potatoes in 125ml olive oil in a non-stick frying pan for about 10 minutes then set the veg aside. Put the turkey and sage into a bowl with some salt and pepper. Beat the eggs and stir them into the turkey mix. Heat 2 tbsp oil in the pan and when hot pour in the turkey mixture so that it covers the pan and then the vegetables. Cook for about 5 minutes or until lightly browned, then turn and repeat on the other side. Start grilling the bacon rashers at the same time as you start heating the oil. Serve by cutting into thick slices with a tablespoon of crème fraîche and crispy bacon rashers on the side.

TURKEY CURRY

4 tbsp vegetable oil ✳ 1 medium onion (chopped) ✳ 4 or 5 garlic
cloves (finely chopped) ✳ 1 tbsp tomato purée ✳ 1 tsp ground cumin
✳ 1 tsp ground coriander ✳ ½ tsp turmeric ✳ ¼ tsp cayenne powder
✳ ¼ tsp garam masala ✳ 1-inch cube of ginger (chopped) ✳ ½ tsp salt
✳ 400–500g roast turkey (in chunks) ✳ 1 tbsp lemon

(If you don't have the garam masala or the turmeric, you can press on
regardless. If you don't have any of the spices, i.e. if you are a student, use
curry powder instead.) Heat 3 tbsp oil in a saucepan and fry the onion
and garlic until the onion has softened and browned
on a medium heat. At the same time, using a
small bowl or cup, mix the tomato purée
with a tablespoon of oil, the cumin,

coriander, turmeric, cayenne, garam
masala, ginger and salt. When you
have a thick paste, stir it into the
onion mixture and fry for about
a minute. Stir in the turkey for a
minute and add 400ml of hot water
from the kettle and let it all simmer
gently for about five minutes. Add the
lemon juice. Garnish with coriander, if
you have any, and serve with basmati rice
and a simple green salad.

HAM AND PEA RISOTTO

25g butter ✳ 350g frozen peas ✳ 200g chopped ham ✳ 1 small
onion, chopped ✳ 1.5 litres hot stock (perhaps from your turkey) ✳
3 teacups risotto rice ✳ Parmesan

Melt the butter, stir in the chopped onion and cook till softened.
Add the chopped ham and the peas and stir for a minute or two. Add
roughly a quarter of the stock and the rice. Let it bubble for a few
minutes and then pour in the rest of the hot stock. Simmer gently. Be
careful not to stir it too much in case you break the peas. If it starts to
dry out, add some more stock or, if you've run out, some hot water
from the kettle. When the rice is cooked, stir in some grated Parmesan.

HOT HAM CAESAR SALAD

Assemble 250g ham sliced into strips, I cos lettuce torn into strips,
I mug of croutons, shavings of Parmesan, a handful of parsley, 4
soft-boiled eggs cut into quarters, 2 or 3 anchovies per serving and
a dollop or two of mayonnaise. Toss the lettuce, croutons, Parmesan
and parsley in the mayonnaise. Flash-fry the slices of ham and lay
them over the lettuce mix with the eggs and the anchovies.

Salads

Below are some simple salad suggestions, using chopped or
shredded turkey:

* *Toss the meat with toasted, unsalted cashews and/or broken walnuts, sliced
  fresh mango or oranges, crumbled Stilton and salad leaves.*

* *Cook thin rice noodles and let them cool. Stir in white turkey meat, some torn
  lettuce, chopped spring onions, shredded carrot and/or cucumber and dress
  with a mixture of soy sauce and sweet chilli sauce.*

* *Cook some couscous and let it cool. Stir through chunks of turkey, diced red
  pepper, canned chickpeas (drained and rinsed), cubes of feta cheese, baby
  tomatoes chopped into halves or quarters and a handful of stoned black olives.*

* *Boil or steam some green beans and
  let them cool. In a bowl, mix them
  with the turkey, some natural
  yoghurt or mayonnaise, lemon
  juice, chopped red peppers and,
  if you want some tang, a
  handful or two
  of crumbled
  Stilton.*

THE VICAR

CHRISTMAS DAY 2006 STARTED FOR ME, AS EVER, WITH THE MIDNIGHT service, which is one of my favourite moments of the year. There's always a fantastic, buzzing atmosphere in the church at this service; an air of joy and anticipation. You can feel the accumulated magic of everyone's childhood memories of Christmas, secular and religious. When it is over and everyone has melted away into the dark, the glow and the thrill are quickly replaced by an eerie 'after-the-party' feel in the echoing silence of the church.

This time, when I walked down through the churchyard and across the road to my home I was surprised to see the lights on. As I shut the door behind me, the kids were just heading upstairs to bed, but my wife Edwina was still hard at work in the kitchen. Our dog Widget had broken into the larder and eaten the entire bowl of bread sauce, all the vegetables she'd prepared and a number of other Christmas goodies. It wasn't until four in the morning that she finally climbed into bed after redoing the whole lot.

I sat up in bed committing to memory the two sermons I was to give in the morning and it was about two thirty when I was happy that it was all safely logged and I could turn out the light.

When the alarm went off at six thirty, I was so tired I had to check I wasn't dead. When I staggered into the bathroom and saw my haggard face staring back at me in the mirror, my belief in the resurrection was strengthened still further! But that's Easter, isn't it? I washed and dressed and, after feeding the pigeons as I do every morning, I drove up to the little church of St Nicholas in the middle of the village to conduct the eight o'clock Christmas Communion service. I was so sleepy it felt like I was having an out-of-body experience at first, but there was a great turnout and by the end it had become a really joyous service. On my way home for breakfast I dropped in at the local post office shop to greet Brian, who gets up earlier than any of us. The rectory was buzzing with activity when I got back. Edwina was shuffling various dishes of food between larder, oven and microwave, the rest of the family were rushing about in various states of undress, and Widget sat in the corner looking sheepish and ashamed. And quite right too.

On to St Mary's, the bigger of the two churches in the parish, for the main ten o'clock service and body and soul were feeling more united now. Again, the church was packed to the rafters and, as at St Nicholas's, the atmosphere was both worshipful and convivial. It felt as if I had shaken hands with half of Sussex by the time the last of the congregation had ambled away. I sat down by the crib for a few moments' peace before heading home, bathing in the wonder of this day when God rolled up his sleeves and entered the world of his own creation. I thought of the Christmas faces of my past, from childhood to the present day, who had all helped make what, for me, is the greatest day in the calendar.

We were just about to sit down at the table when a parishioner called in with the alarming news that a gravestone had been dug up and taken away. With my heart racing and a lump in my throat, I headed straight up to the churchyard. Sure enough, the stone of someone who had been buried only a few weeks earlier was indeed missing. It must have been vandals, I thought, but just to make sure before calling the police I rang the stonemason. 'Blast it! I forgot to tell you,' he said apologetically. 'I took it away yesterday to work on over the Christmas break. I meant to call you!' Panic over.

The dinner was delayed but it was worth the wait because Edwina had done us proud. In spite of Widget's best efforts to ruin the day, it was a wonderful occasion as neighbours joined the family for the meal. After exchanging gifts, playing some games in the sitting room and taking our guests home, I went up to bed at about ten thirty. I sat up for a while going over the events of the day in my head and, after kissing Edwina good night, a profound thought struck me. Widget had eaten everything he could find in the larder — except the Brussels sprouts. Even dogs hate Brussels sprouts! I smiled and rolled over. Wow, I love Christmas!

THE REVD CANON DAVID PARKER, parish of Lavant

Bring in the Trees:

The Origins of Christmas Traditions

THE SOUND OF DISGRUNTLED PEOPLE BLEATING INTO THEIR BEARDS and teacups about the reduced role of Christianity in modern Christmas celebrations has been humming in the background for so long now that it has almost become a Christmas custom in its own right. Perhaps it is a tradition that we should preserve for future generations because, like all our other Christmas customs, it has virtually nothing to do with honouring the birth of Christ. It is a fact, as plain as the boil on the end of my nose, and one well worth passing on to the louder Christmas carpers in our midst, that every significant Christmas tradition we practise today, bar building a Nativity scene, has its origins not in Christian teaching, let alone the Bible, but in ancient pagan customs or nineteenth-century commercial initiatives. Bringing a Christmas tree into the home, kissing under the mistletoe, exchanging gifts, indulging in a large feast, throwing parties, lighting up the street with colourful illumi-nations, decorating the house with holly and ivy, hunting on Boxing Day, lighting candles, burning the Yule log, eating sausages and bacon with our turkey, setting the Christmas pudding ablaze – these are all versions of customs practised for centuries by our pre-Christian ancestors. (Sending Christmas cards and pulling crackers, meanwhile, have nothing to do with Christianity *or* paganism. They are the inventions of enterprising Victorians.) The truth is that the

early Church authorities quickly realized that Christianity had a better chance of surviving and thriving if they incorporated into the Christian experience those wintertime pagan rituals which, for thousands of years, had formed a central part of so many European cultures. If they forced a break with the pre-Christian past, the Church risked alienating the very people they were so desperately trying to convert or to keep on board.

SOME CHURCHES IN BRITAIN CONTINUE TO **FORBID THE USE OF mistletoe** in Christmas decorations. The early Christian Church in Britain was willing to ignore or even embrace other pagan customs, but it made great efforts to ban the use of mistletoe because of its strong associations with the powerful Druids. The Church suggested holly as an evergreen alternative, claiming that the plant's sharp leaves represented the thorns of Christ's crown on the cross and the berries were the drops of his blood. In Brittany mistletoe is known as *Herbe de la Croix* because it was believed that Christ's cross was made from the wood. According to the Breton legend, mistletoe was once a tree but was reduced to a parasite after the crucifixion.

❄ ❄ ❄ ❄

SCANDINAVIAN LORE HAS AN EXPLANATION FOR how mistletoe ended up at the top of trees. The legend goes that Frigga, wife of Odin and goddess of love and beauty, banished the mistletoe to the forest canopy after her son, Balder the Beautiful, was slain by a dart made from its wood. When Balder came back to life three days later, Frigga made mistletoe a symbol of **love and eternal life**.

❄ ❄ ❄ ❄

THE CUSTOM OF **KISSING UNDER THE MISTLETOE** HAS ITS ANCIENT origins in our ancestors' belief that the plant conferred powers of fertility and vitality. Some even considered it an aphrodisiac, owing to the allegedly sexual nature of the plant (Y-shaped branches, white sticky juice of ball-shaped berries — in fact, let's not go there). As recently as late medieval times, women were in the habit of wrapping mistletoe around their waist and wrists to increase their chances of conceiving. This belief arose partly from the fact that, like other evergreens, mistletoe's life force was so strong that it could live through the harshest of winters and even produce fruit. The mistletoe's way of reproducing and surviving without any roots in the ground led ancient Britons to believe it had magical properties. On closer scientific inspection, however, there is little that might be considered 'sexy' in the way the plant goes about the business of reproducing. In fact, it's about as erotic as a bucket of iced water down a naked back: mistletoe reproduces itself through bird shit. This is how it works: birds swallow plant's berries, birds crap on branch, seeds in droppings germinate in the bark, mistletoe grows, and excitable, unenlightened pagan ancestors jump up and down, grunting something unintelligible along the lines of 'Blimey, that plant's grown out of nothing!' Sometimes the process begins when the birds (often the mistle thrush) finish gorging themselves on the berries and find their beaks covered in sticky juice, which they proceed to wipe off on the bark of the tree. Mistletoe takes its name from this very process of reproduction, *mistel* being the Anglo-Saxon word for dung and *tan* the word for small branch.

✳ ✳ ✳ ✳

It is hard to say exactly what is the origin of the English 'kissing under the mistletoe', but the practice would appear to be due to an imagined relation between the love of the sexes and the spirit of fertility embodied in the sacred bough, and it may be a vestige of the licence often permitted at folk-festivals. According to one form of the English custom the young men plucked, each time they kissed a girl, a berry from the bough. When the berries were all picked, the privilege ceased.

WASHINGTON IRVING
The Sketch Book, 1819–20

✳ ✳ ✳ ✳

The birthplace of the Christmas-Tree is Egypt, and its origin dates from a period long antecedent to the Christian era. The palm-tree is known to put forth a shoot every month and a spray of this tree with twelve shoots on it was used in Egypt at the time of the winter solstice as a symbol of the year completed. The palm-tree spray of Egypt, on reaching Italy, became a branch of any other tree (the tip of the fir was found most suitable from its pyramidal or conical shape) and was decorated with burning tapers lit in honour of Saturn, whose saturnalia were celebrated from the 17th to the 21st of December, the period of the winter solstice.

Illustrated London News, December 1854

EVERGREEN TREES HAVE BEEN USED TO CELEBRATE PAGAN WINTER festivals for thousands of years. In northern Europe, the fir tree was the most common evergreen, and our ancestors used branches of fir to decorate their homes from the winter solstice through to spring. Evergreens were seen as symbols of eternal life at a time of year when all other forms of plant life had died off or gone into hibernation. The people of southern Europe – and beyond – also venerated evergreens during the winter months. The Romans used fir trees to decorate their temples during the rowdy December festival of Saturnalia. The Christians **commandeered the evergreen tradition**, and turned its symbolism of everlasting life to their own theological advantage.

❄ ❄ ❄ ❄

THE FIRST REFERENCES IN PRINT TO CHRISTMAS TREES COME FROM Germany in the early sixteenth century, but Riga, the capital of Latvia, likes to claim that its citizens erected the first tree in public in the year 1510. Not much is known about the erection of the Riga tree other than that men in black hats turned up, held a short ceremony of an indeterminate nature and then promptly burned the tree – which doesn't sound very Christmassy. My money's on the Germans.

❄ ❄ ❄ ❄

INDEED, ALL TRAILS LEAD BACK TO GERMANY WHEN YOU TRY TO HUNT down the origins of the Christmas tree. As with so many Christmas customs, it is **impossible to say** exactly when, how and why the fir tree came to be used as a central feature of Christmas decorations. But it is clear that there were stirrings in the snow-covered forests of the German territories, and the sound of axe upon bark, long before the rest of the Christian world had thought about bringing an entire tree into their home. The PR department of the Lutheran Church – or at least its sixteenth- or seventeenth-century equivalent – liked to claim that it was Martin Luther himself, the German founder of Protestantism, who first came up with the idea of having a decorated tree in the home. The story goes that Martin was stumbling through some wintry woods looking at the stars twinkling through the snow-dusted fir trees when, Eureka! the penny dropped. Why not chop one of these chaps down, he thought, and cover it with candles in honour of Christ's birth? Nice try, but I think not. There is not a scrap of historical documentation to back up this claim, so the most likely explanation is that the introduction of the Christmas tree was merely the logical extension of the pagan custom of bringing branches of evergreens into the home.

As German royals married into other European dynasties in the eighteenth and nineteenth centuries, they brought with them many of the customs of their homeland. The first reference to a Christmas tree in the British royal household comes in the reign of the Hanoverian George III, when his German-born wife, Queen Charlotte, is credited with its introduction at Windsor Castle in the late 1700s. A contemporary account describes *A fir tree, about as high again as any of us, lighted all over with small tapers, several little wax dolls among the branches in different places, and strings of almonds and raisins alternately tied from one to the other, with skipping ropes for the boys, and each bigger girl had muslin for a frock, a muslin handkerchief, and a fan, and a sash, all prettily done up in a handkerchief, and a pretty necklace and earrings besides.*

❄ ❄ ❄ ❄

It wasn't until around 1850 that Christmas trees became a common-place feature in British homes. Following his marriage in 1840 to Queen Victoria, the German nobleman Albert of Saxe-Coburg and Gotha was keen to import some German customs into the royal household, particularly at Christmas, which he regarded as a special time for the family. Victoria was only too happy to make him feel at home and before long Windsor Castle was **ablaze with giant fir trees**, dripping with gifts, confectionery and dozens of carefully placed tapers. Today we take Christmas trees for granted but they must have been a spectacular and thrilling sight for the couple's young children. In 1848, an illustration of the royal family gathered around their decorated tree was published in the popular *Illustrated London News*. Within a few years every middle-class family worth its name would have a Christmas tree of their own.

❄ ❄ ❄ ❄

It is that childish, open-hearted simplicity which, so it seems to me, makes Christmas essentially German, or at any rate explains why it is that nowhere else in the world does it find so pure an expression. The German is himself simple, warm-hearted, unpretentious, with something at the bottom of him which is childlike in the best sense. He is the last 'Naturmensch' [child of nature] in civilization. Christmas suits him as well as a play suits an actor for whose character and temperament it has been especially written.

Ms I. A. R. Wylie
My German Year, 1910

HANDEL'S *MESSIAH* HAS LONG BEEN associated with Christmas but the famous oratorio was written as a piece for Easter. Handel, depressed and in debt at the time, was approached by his friend Charles Jenners to compose an oratorio based on Jenners's own recent arrangement of the Scriptures. Handel shelved his plans to return to his native Germany and, working from his home at 25 Brook Street in his adopted London, wrote the entire work in a remarkable **24-day burst** at the end of the summer of 1741. 'I did think I did see all Heaven before me and the great God himself,' Handel said of its composition. The *Messiah* was first performed in Dublin in April the following year.

❄ ❄ ❄ ❄

A Christmas tree may be made at home for a very trifling cost. Long as they have been in fashion in England for juvenile parties, or for Christmas Eve, these trees seem to be still in favour almost as much as ever. Christmas trees may be covered with paltry trifles, or made the medium for dispensing suitable gifts amongst the members of the household ... The ordinary Christmas tree is covered with miscellaneous articles, some of more value than others, which are either distributed at hazard by the lady deputed to cut them down, or lots are drawn out of a bag of numbers corresponding to those fixed on the little presents themselves.

Cassell's Book of the Household, 1878

❄ ❄ ❄ ❄

SLADE'S 'MERRY XMAS EVERYBODY' WAS THE CHRISTMAS NUMBER ONE of 1973, beating Wizzard's 'I Wish It Could Be Christmas Every Day' into fourth place, but it was actually written six years earlier under the title 'Buy Me A Rocking Chair'. Lead singer Noddy Holder, who wrote the song with bass guitarist Jim Lea, said they wanted to lift the mood of the country, which had been brought low by economic depression and social unrest. (Not to mention Victorian sideburns, multi-pocketed polyester flared trousers with eight buttons on an elasticated waist and sandwich spread.) 'I wanted it to be a working-class British Christmas song, with all the political and social stuff going on at the time,' Holder said. 'It was very grim: there was the three-day week, power cuts in the evening, there was a miners' strike. The country couldn't have been at a lower ebb.'

When rosemary, and bays, the poet's crown,
Are bawl'd in frequent cries through all the town,
Then judge the festival of Christmas near,
Christmas, the joyous period of the year.
Now with bright holly all your temples strow,
With laurel green and sacred mistletoe.
Now, heav'n-born Charity, thy blessings shed;
Bid meagre Want uprear her sickly head:
Bid shiv'ring limbs be warm; let plenty's bowl
In humble roofs make glad the needy soul.

JOHN GAY (1685–1732)
Trivia, or the Art of Walking the Streets of London

❅ ❅ ❅ ❅

'HUNTING THE WREN' IS ONE OF THE MORE UNFATHOMABLE CHRISTMAS customs practised over the centuries by the British and Irish (and French to a lesser extent). Dozens of historians and folklore experts have failed to produce a satisfactory explanation of its meaning or origins. It has all but died out in England but it is still practised in remote pockets of Ireland. Customs varied from country to country, district to district and century to century, but they were all versions of the same theme. During the Christmas period, the men of the village or town, sometimes in costume, would set out to kill a wren and fasten its body to the top of a long pole. They carried it in procession to all the houses, singing a special song and demanding money or a gift. In Ireland, one of the many variations of the song begins:

The wren, the wren, the king of all birds,
On St Stephen's Day was caught in the furze,
Although he is little, his family is great,
I pray you, good landlady, give us a treat.

When every house had been visited, the procession headed to the churchyard where the wren was buried in a solemn ceremony. Historians suspect that the origins of this custom are as old as any in our culture, stretching back many centuries, even millennia, before the Christian era. The most plausible explanation goes like this: the little wren is known as 'the king of birds', and for many centuries it was considered highly sacred. To kill one was regarded as the height of bad luck — except during the winter solstice, when it was customary for our primitive ancestors to slaughter a divine animal.

❄ ❄ ❄ ❄

The time-honoured epoch for taking down Christmas decorations from Church and house is Candlemas Day, February 2nd. Terribly withered they are by that time. Candlemas in old times represented the end of the Christmas holidays, which, when 'fine old leisure' reigned, were far longer than they are now. Every particle ought to be removed long before for cleanliness' sake, and not, as old Herrick puts it, because —

For how many leaves there be,
So many goblins you shall see

But when decorations were kept up till Candlemas in those merry old times, there was no gas, nor was the atmosphere of the house heated as it is today; there were too many chinks and crevices for that. It is found desirable now, in many houses, to remove them after Twelfth Day, January 6th (the Epiphany or Jour Des Rois); and by that time they are quite dusty and dirty enough, and everybody (except the children) is tired of holiday-making and ready to return to the sober business of life.

Cassell's Book of the Household, 1878

❄ ❄ ❄ ❄

FAIRY LIGHTS BEGAN TO APPEAR IN SHOP WINDOWS IN ABOUT 1900 but it wasn't until after the Second World War that the majority of households could afford them.

❄ ❄ ❄ ❄

IN 1941, NOT LONG AFTER THE ATTACK ON PEARL HARBOR, UK Prime Minister Sir Winston Churchill stood side by side with Franklin Roosevelt outside the White House for the **annual lighting of the national tree**. There was no ceremony the following two years owing to wartime electricity restrictions. In 1963, Lyndon Johnson delayed the start of the ceremony until a 30-day period of mourning for the assassinated John F. Kennedy had passed. In 1979, Jimmy Carter cancelled the ceremony in honour of the Americans being held hostage in Iran. The following year he ordered it lit for just 417 seconds — one for every day the hostages had been held.

I have been looking on, this evening, at a merry company of children assembled round that pretty German toy, a Christmas Tree. The tree was planted in the middle of a great round table, and towered high above their heads. It was brilliantly lighted by a multitude of little tapers; and everywhere sparkled and glittered with bright objects. There were rosy-cheeked dolls, hiding behind the green leaves; and there were real watches (with movable hands, at least, and an endless capacity of being wound up) dangling from innumerable twigs; there were French-polished tables, chairs, bedsteads, wardrobes, eight-day clocks, and various other articles of domestic furniture (wonderfully made, in tin, at Wolverhampton), perched among the boughs, as if in preparation for some fairy housekeeping; there were jolly, broad-faced little men, much more agreeable in appearance than many real men — and no wonder, for their heads took off, and showed them to be full of sugar-plums; there were fiddles and drums; there were tambourines, books, work-boxes, paint-boxes, sweetmeat-boxes, peep-show boxes, and all kinds of boxes; there were trinkets for the elder girls, far brighter than any grown-up gold and jewels; there were baskets and pincushions in all devices; there were guns, swords, and banners; there were witches standing in enchanted rings of pasteboard, to tell fortunes; there were teetotums, humming-tops, needle-cases, pen-wipers, smelling-bottles, conversation-cards, bouquet-holders; real fruit, made artificially dazzling with gold leaf; imitation

apples, pears, and walnuts, crammed with surprises; in short, as a pretty child, before me, delightedly whispered to another pretty child, her bosom friend, 'There was everything, and more.' This motley collection of odd objects, clustering on the tree like magic fruit, and flashing back the bright looks directed towards it from every side – some of the diamond-eyes admiring it were hardly on a level with the table, and a few were languishing in timid wonder on the bosoms of pretty mothers, aunts, and nurses – made a lively realisation of the fancies of childhood; and set me thinking how all the trees that grow and all the things that come into existence on the earth, have their wild adornments at that well-remembered time.

Being now at home again, and alone, the only person in the house awake, my thoughts are drawn back, by a fascination which I do not care to resist, to my own childhood. I begin to consider, what do we all remember best upon the branches of the Christmas Tree of our own young Christmas days, by which we climbed to real life. Straight, in the middle of the room, cramped in the freedom of its growth by no encircling walls or soon-reached ceiling, a shadowy tree arises; and, looking up into the dreamy brightness of its top – for I observe in this tree the singular property that it appears to grow downward towards the earth – I look into my youngest Christmas recollections!...

Among the later toys and fancies hanging there – as idle often and less pure – be the images once associated with the sweet old Waits, the softened music in the night, ever unalterable! Encircled by the social thoughts of Christmas-time, still let the benignant figure of my childhood stand unchanged! In every cheerful image and suggestion that the season brings, may the bright star that rested above the poor roof, be the star of all the Christian World! A moment's pause, O vanishing tree, of which the lower boughs are dark to me as yet, and let me look once more! I know there are blank spaces on thy branches, where eyes that I have loved have shone and smiled; from which they are departed. But, far above, I see the raiser of the dead girl, and the Widow's Son; and God is good! If Age be hiding for me in the unseen portion of thy downward growth, O may I, with a grey head, turn a child's heart to that figure yet, and a child's trustfulness and confidence!

Now, the tree is decorated with bright merriment, and song, and dance, and cheerfulness. And they are welcome. Innocent and welcome be they ever held, beneath the branches of the Christmas Tree, which cast no gloomy shadow! But, as it sinks into the ground, I hear a whisper going through the leaves. 'This, in commemoration of the law of love and kindness, mercy and compassion. This, in remembrance of Me!'

CHARLES DICKENS
A Christmas Tree, 1850

AS YOU SETTLE DOWN TO WRITE YOUR 87TH CHRISTMAS CARD, WITH
the clock striking midnight and the repetitive strain injury starting
to bite, you can cheer yourself up by cursing the name of Sir Henry
Cole. (Damn your eyes, Cole! Damn your eyes, Cole!) Cole was
one of those restless Victorian enthusiasts who didn't like to put his
feet up at the end of a day until a) he had invented something or b)
he had founded or constructed something or c) he had reformed
something. After an early career in the Public Records Office (which
he reformed, of course), Cole became a very busy man indeed. In
1850, as an active member of the Royal Academy, he took on the role
of principal organizer of the Great Exhibition, a year later he was
appointed Prince Albert's chief adviser, and for the rest of the decade
he oversaw the foundation of what is now the Victoria and Albert
Museum. He was also the man responsible for the introduction of
public lavatories in England. It's amazing he found the time to go to
the loo. Earlier, in December 1842, when the onus of reinventing
Western civilization began to mount on his broad shoulders, Cole
became frustrated that there was no time left in his manic schedule
to send letters offering festive greetings to all his friends … so he
invented the printed Christmas card. The cards were designed and
printed by someone else and he simply scribbled his signature at the
bottom. Bingo! At a stroke he had freed up a few more days to found,
reform and invent things. Cole commissioned artist John Calcott
Horsley to design a card for him, which featured a slightly drunk-
looking family raising a toast around a table, surrounded by a border
of more worthy images of people feeding the poor and clothing the
naked and so on. Just over 1,000 were printed and those that Sir
Henry did not need were sold for one shilling.

❄ ❄ ❄ ❄

WITH THE INTRODUCTION OF THE 'PENNY POST' IN 1840 AND
the modernization of the printing industry, the practice
of **sending Christmas cards** began to catch on amongst
the middle classes, but it wasn't until the 1860s that the
cards were widely sold on the market. And it wasn't until the 1870s
that the custom of sending one to every single person in the family
address book, including the milkman, the dustman and the funny-
looking chap who delivers the logs, was firmly established.

❄ ❄ ❄ ❄

ONE STRANGE ENGLISH CHRISTMAS CUSTOM THAT HAS FALLEN INTO
disuse is the baking of the **Dumb Cake.** On Christmas Eve, a single

girl wanting to discover her future husband prepared a cake, alone and in silence. She pricked the mixture with her initials and then left it in her bedroom before going to sleep with her door open. At midnight her husband-to-be was supposed to enter the room and leave his initials on the cake, and the girl would bake it the following morning. It's a wonder that custom ever died out.

❄ ❄ ❄ ❄

THE NEXT TIME YOU LIGHT THE BRANDY ON THE CHRISTMAS PUDDING, light a Christmas candle, wrap your tree in fairy lights, burn a Christmas log or watch your local street illuminations being turned on, remember that you are continuing a winter tradition that stretches back to the very dawn of civilization. These **light and fire traditions** have become such an entrenched feature of Christmas that we have ceased to question why and how they have come to play such a central role. The answer, like so many, lies with our pagan ancestors and not with the teachings of the Church. During the winter solstice, fires were lit all over northern Europe to honour the rising of the sun and the lengthening of the days. People living off the fruit of the land worshipped the returning sun because it gave them the food they needed to live. At the same time as their northern cousins, the Romans also celebrated the winter solstice with the feast of Natalis Invicti Solis. In the east of the Roman Empire, the worship of the sun was equally widespread and formed the essence of the cult of Mithraism, which rivalled Christianity in the early days. The sun-god cult bore great resemblances to Christianity and was eventually absorbed by it.

Christmas-related Cockney rhyming slang

Mince pies — *Eyes*
Christmas Eve — *Believe*
Christmas crackered — *Knackered*
Turtle doves — *Gloves*
Morecambe and Wise — *Flies*
Brussels sprouts — *Scouts*
Elephant's trunk — *Drunk*
Box of toys — *Noise*
Big dippers or kippers — *Slippers*
Wobbly jelly — *Telly*
Plates and dishes — *Missis*

Stand at ease — *Cheese*
Sugar candy — *Handy*
Tom and Dick — *Sick*
Dustbin lids — *Kids*
Emma Freuds — *Haemorrhoids*
Fine and dandy — *Brandy*
Left in the lurch — *Church*
Pinky and Perky — *Turkey*
Schindler's List — *Pissed*
Wallace and Gromit — *Vomit*
Vera Lynn — *Gin*
Plates of meat — *Feet*

How **BOXING DAY** CAME TO ACQUIRE ITS NAME IS A MATTER OF MINOR dispute among historians and etymologists. From Victorian times until fairly recently, 26 December was the day on which better-off households gave gifts to servants, tradesmen and the local poor, often presented in boxes. (The modern practice of giving Christmas bonuses to employees is thought to be an extension of this custom.) Another theory contends that the name dates back to the late Middle Ages when alms boxes were placed in churches for the collection of donations, which were handed to the poor on the day after Christmas. Boxing Day is an institution of the British Commonwealth and is not recognized or kept in the United States or elsewhere. In the UK, Australia and Canada, it developed into a public holiday from the old tradition of giving servants the day off, in recognition of all the work they put in during the preparation of the Christmas Day celebrations. ('There we go, Miss Atkins, you have a nice lie-down today, and here's a box of candied carrots in gratitude for the 23-hour days you've been working for the past three months ...')

❋ ❋ ❋ ❋

ST STEPHEN BECAME THE FIRST CHRISTIAN MARTYR AFTER HE WAS stoned to death by crowds in Jerusalem for speaking against the Temple and the Law. He is the **patron saint of horses** and his feast day falls on 26 December, which explains Boxing Day's ancient association with horse activities. In Germany horses were once ridden around churches on St Stephen's Day and in parts of England men bled them to encourage good health for the coming year. Today, hunts and race meetings continue the traditions.

THE TRADITION OF EATING **TWELFTH NIGHT CAKE**, now virtually extinct in Britain, was for centuries a central feature of our Christmas celebrations. The cook mixed various items into a rich fruitcake, each of which said something about the people who found them. If you found the dry bean, you were the king or queen; if you got the clove, you were a crook; if you got the twig you were a fool and if you were served the rag you were, er, a slag. Nowadays, the cook may place a coin in the Christmas pudding, to be served on Christmas Day. The tradition of the Twelfth Night Cake — minus the extra ingredients — is still maintained by the Drury Lane Theatre. In his will, an eighteenth-century English actor called Robert Baddeley bequeathed three pounds per annum to provide wine and cake to feed 'Her Majesty's Company of Comedians' in the green-room of the theatre on Twelfth Night.

❄ ❄ ❄ ❄

THE TRADITION OF BUYING **POINSETTIAS** AS POT PLANTS AT CHRISTMAS time comes from Mexico, via the United States. Native to southern Mexico, Central America and Africa, they are named after Joel Roberts Poinsett, the first American ambassador to Mexico, who started importing them to the States in the late 1820s. There are all sorts of Latin American Christian legends about how the plant has come to be associated so closely with Christmas. But these are all nonsense and you should politely look the other way or, if you must, leave the room when someone starts to spout off about Mexican infants weeping tears of blood under a roadside plant on 25 December ... The plain truth is that poinsettias look good at Christmas time: they flower in the winter and happen to come in red and green, the traditional colours of Christmas.

❄ ❄ ❄ ❄

UNTIL RECENT YEARS, THREE GENERATIONS OF THE ECKE FAMILY (Paul Sr, Paul Jr, Paul III) of Encinitas, California, enjoyed a **near-monopoly** in the poinsettia market, because they were privy to a horticultural secret that left their competitors floundering to keep up. The Eckes developed a technique of grafting two varieties together to create fuller, leafier plants with more branches than the originals. The Eckes managed to keep their technique within the family business for almost 60 years until university researchers in the mid-1990s discovered it for themselves and went public with their findings.

CHRISTMAS TREES ARE **GETTING SHORTER**, ACCORDING TO RECENT research by the University of Cambridge. After spraying spruce trees with various compounds over a three-year period, researchers found that the plants treated with nitrogen were significantly shorter and wider and more densely branched than the others. Higher nitrogen levels, found in common agricultural treatments such as fertilizers and animal sewage, stimulate a hormone called cytokinin. The hormone causes buds to grow from the stem and become branches, so trees start to grow outwards as well as upwards, stunting their normal height.

✱   ✱   ✱   ✱

THE CHRISTMAS CRACKER WAS INVENTED IN THE 1840S BY A HIGHLY ambitious English baker called Tom Smith. When he was old enough to set up his own business, the enterprising Smith travelled to Paris in search of new confectionery ideas. 'Bon-bons', sweets wrapped in twists of coloured paper, were popular in the French capital at the time and Smith returned to England with a cunning plan: his own 'bon-bons' would contain a love motto. After the novelty sweets went on sale in 1847, Smith continued to develop his idea, dumping the candy, adding small gimmicky toys, lengthening the wrapper and, after exhaustive experimentation, adding **little explosive strips** which popped when pulled. The crackers, originally called 'cosaques', quickly gained in popularity and were used at all manner of special events and occasions, not just Christmas. Smith's son Walter is credited with the introduction of paper hats as well as the replacement of love messages with witty sayings.

There has been an awful lot of rubbish written about how the custom of the **Christmas stocking** originally came into being. The most irksome version, and one of the most frequently circulated, involves St Nicholas, the fourth-century Turkish bishop, who later turned into Santa Claus. It goes like this: once upon a time, a kindly nobleman, distraught over the death of his wife, squandered his fortune, leaving his three daughters without dowries and facing a life of spinsterhood. Hearing of the girls' plight, St Nick immediately mounted his white horse and rode like the wind to offer help. Keen to remain anonymous, for reasons unexplained, St Nick hurtled by the nobleman's house and threw three pouches of gold coins into the air. Incredibly, all three of the pouches flew straight down the chimney and, even more incredibly, they somehow landed in three stockings that the three daughters just happened to have hung by the fireplace to dry. Sherlock Holmes, no doubt, would begin his investigation by asking: why three stockings, not six? Had the girls spent the day at a Turkish hopping competition in the local marsh? Call me cynical if you wish, but you try running the 'St Nick stocking legend' past your seven-year-old child. You will be met with a face of stony incredulity. The most plausible explanation of the stocking seems to be that in various European countries, it was the custom to leave out some kind of receptacle (clog/sock/pouch) over the Christmas period, which was filled either by St Nicholas, the patron saint of children (or some other Christian manifestation), or by some variation on the theme of a Christmas or winter spirit (fairy/troll/gnome/nice witch). In the early nineteenth century, the stocking beat off its rivals to become the preferred present receptacle of young children. This may have had something to do with the fact that a stocking can hold more gifts than a sock, and that the Dutch fashion of wearing uncomfortable wooden shoes never really caught on elsewhere. It's more likely, however, that Clement Clark Moore's reference to stockings in his famous poem 'Twas the Night Before Christmas' and Thomas Nast's subsequent illustrations of the poem simply popularized a custom that, up until then, was little known and practised by only a few.

THE RACEHORSE TRAINER

EVERY DAY IS A WORKING DAY FOR ME – ALL 365 OF THEM – AND
Christmas Day is just like any other. The horses need feeding and
exercising and the stables need mucking out. Horses never give you
the day off. Also, Boxing Day is traditionally one of the big racing
days of the year, and if we have any runners, they need to be given
a good go on the gallops the day before. I realized last year (2006)
that I have worked every Christmas Day for half a century. The needs
of horses have changed little over the years, and virtually nothing in
the way we look after them has changed since my father first started
training racehorses back in 1955. We feed them, they shit, we clear it
out, we give them fresh bedding, and take them out for a gallop.

I began by helping out my dad as a five-year-old, mucking out the
stables and preparing the horse feed. I'd open the presents in my
stocking from Father Christmas and then, at first light, my brother
John and I would get dressed and head down the road to the stables
with Dad. At the end of the morning, we'd get cleaned up and dressed
for Christmas lunch with the family, and then, with a bellyful of
turkey and pudding, it was back down to the stables to tend to the
horses in the afternoon. Young horses need their exercise, so it's a
nightmare if it has snowed or there's been a hard frost because we can't
take them out into the fields for a gallop. We have a small exercise
circle about 20 feet in diameter, but you can only do one horse at a
time and they can't go round it faster than a trot.

Fortunately it doesn't snow much in the south of England these
days, but I remember the incredible winter of 1962/63 when a
snowstorm blew in on Boxing Day, and the temperature dropped
sharply. It didn't thaw out for three months. The lanes around the
village were often filled with drifts as high as the hedges. I remember
one of the horses getting stuck in a drift after leaping a fence and
sinking up to her head in snow. Dad had a hell of a job dragging
her out. As a young boy, that winter was a fantastic time. We missed
a lot of school and spent day after day sledging on the South Downs
and having snowball fights. Dad wasn't so happy about it, though,
because it meant that the horses didn't get their exercise. He kept
hoping the big thaw would come, but it wasn't until April that
the ground was finally free. Almost all the race meetings across
the country were cancelled, from Boxing Day pretty well until the
Cheltenham Festival in early spring.

I remember vividly going down to the stables with Dad as a young boy on Christmas Day, but since I was a teenager it's just a blur, one day being no different from any other. There is one Christmas Day, however, that I will never forget. It was in the mid-1980s and I was down at the stables finishing off my work for the morning when I heard a bit of a commotion on the road outside. I went out to see what was going on, and was met by the slightly alarming sight of about 50 cows careering through the narrow lane that leads into the heart of the village. Someone had left a gate open and the herd had just wandered out of the field and headed up along the road, past the pub and the stables and through the village, crashing into front gardens, trampling and munching them to destruction.

I immediately called the farmer and then went to see if I could help him herd them into somewhere safe until he decided what to do. With hindsight, I wish I'd gone home instead! The pressure of the rest of the herd had forced some of the cows into the big slurry pit halfway up the lane, and one of them had gone in so deep she had got stuck and was starting to get distressed. There was no way she was going to get out on her own, so I went back to the village and called the Fire Brigade. Somehow we had to get a belt around the cow so they could drag her out with the winch.

I'm still not too sure why it was me who ended up wading into that giant pool of muck and not the farmer or one of the firemen. I think the farmer had a bad back or something, and the firemen said they weren't used to dealing with cattle! That left Muggins. It was a proper nightmare. By the time I got to the cow and started to strap the belt around her I was up to my armpits in runny shit. The smell was horrendous. Gagging all the time, I finally managed to get the belt on and the firemen were able slowly to drag the cow clear. I walked the half-mile or so home, looking like a swamp monster. The turkey had just been taken from the oven when I walked into the house. 'Merry Christmas!' I said to my wife Sally. She just looked at me and said: 'Maybe you should get changed before we sit down for lunch.'

STEVE WOODMAN, racehorse trainer

Turkey in the Trenches:

Christmas at War

ACCORDING TO THE MEDIEVAL code of chivalry, all warring factions were obliged to down their weapons over the Christmas period. By 1460, this honourable tradition appears to have fallen into disuse as Lancastrians and Yorkists butchered one other in the Battle of Wakefield on 30 December. It was during this especially bloody battle of the Wars of the Roses, a victory for the Lancastrians, that Richard

"HELLO, SANTA!"
Sgt. Will Neil, 10th Black Watch.

Duke of York and his son, the 12-year-old Earl of Rutland, were killed and their bodies violated by the savage Lord

Clifford in acts so hideous that they swung public sympathy towards the Yorkist claim to the throne. After the Duke was killed, Clifford cut off his head, put a paper crown on top and then stuck it on a pole and exhibited it on the city walls of York. Later, he caught up with the fugitive Earl of Rutland, and stabbed the pre-pubescent boy in the heart as he begged for mercy. His head found its way on to a pole alongside his father's.

❋ ❋ ❋ ❋

AS THE LUFTWAFFE INTENSIFIED its bombing blitz on London and other British cities in late 1940, *Good Housekeeping* magazine showed a flash of humour by suggesting readers made their Christmas cakes in the shape of an **Anderson air-raid shelter**.

❋ ❋ ❋ ❋

Xmas Day. I must give an account of how we spent Xmas in camp. A good many of us received parcels from home containing cakes and puddings etc. These were heroically put on one side, until Xmas Day, then each man

who had anything took a chum who had not received anything and shared with him, so that every man had a little taste of the homeland. On Xmas Eve there was a heavy fall of snow and Xmas morning we awoke to a fine morning and three or four inches on the ground. Then the fun started. The English and French formed sides against the Russians and then commenced a right battle royal. First the English rushed the Russian lines, with a terrible shout, the same shout doing more to dishearten the enemy than the actual snowballs. Charging and counter-charging was the order all the morning. For myself I have started to hold a series of Church of England services in a large empty tent. I was fortunate enough to get around 100 hymn books through the American Ambassador Mr Gerrard at Berlin and these series of services are a great boon to the camp.

PTE THOMAS RAINBIRD
Letter home from Doberitz prisoner-of-war camp, January 1915

❋ ❋ ❋ ❋

Winston Churchill had left Egypt on 11 December 1943 to fly home after the historic conferences with Allied war leaders at Cairo and Teheran. From that moment there had been a complete clamp-down on any news of his whereabouts.

He left Cairo intending to meet General Eisenhower at Tunis but his aircraft encountered an extraordinary series of blunders. The Prime Minister had left Cairo suffering from extreme exhaustion and by the following morning he was desperately ill with pneumonia.

When he rose from his bed ten days later, his mind was fully occupied with the Allied landing at Anzio. The naval Commander-in-Chief, Mediterranean, was bombarded with demands for information on the availability of Landing Craft for that invasion. As the Flag Lieutenant, I was instructed to accompany Admiral Sir John Cunningham to see the Prime Minister.

When we arrived at Mr Churchill's headquarters we were joined by the top brass of the Mediterranean theatre headed by General Eisenhower, General Bedell-Smith, General Sir Henry Maitland-Wilson and Air Marshal Sir Arthur Tedder.

Mrs Churchill was there with daughter Sarah, her son Randolph and the Prime Minister's physician, Lord Moran. I also recognized Mr Churchill's watchdog, Detective Inspector Thomson, and met 'Tommy' Thompson, Churchill's 'personal assistant', and Desmond Morton, his 'special investigator'.

As the most junior officer present, I decided to move into the only unoccupied corner before anyone asked me searching questions. Then Mr Churchill entered the room, shook my hand, and inquired, 'How are you on this glorious Christmas morning? I have asked you and several other young officers here today because I thought you might have a more

"The Knave of Spades."

said. 'It was touch and go. When he was in a critical state he said to me, "Thompson, if this is the end it is well that I should die in sight of Carthage."'

At dinner Mr Churchill dined in his bedroom with his senior guests but afterwards he returned to talk to the rest. His entry into the room produced a remarkable effect with everyone, including the most eminent Generals and Air Marshals, assuming an air of rigid and deferential alertness, and stammering halting replies to any questions he asked. It took me back to my schooldays. At any moment any of us from Eisenhower, the head of the school, to Pawle, the most junior new boy, might be confronted with some shocking neglect of duty by the new headmaster.

But on that Christmas night so many years ago Winston Churchill seemed only concerned that for all his guests and particularly the younger officers, this should be an occasion they would recall all their lives.

I was to see Mr Churchill many times again. I was even to write a book about him with the great man's blessing. But that first Christmas meeting on the shores of the Bay of Tunis, when he returned from the shadows to take a leading part in the making of history, was the most memorable of all.

agreeable Christmas with me than you would in your Algerian fastness.' He then left the room and a surprising number of complete strangers gathered around me, convinced that Mr Churchill had imparted some information of great importance, and I saw no reason to disillusion them.

When lunch time arrived we were sharply deflated. While the rest of the guests filed into the dining room we were banished to a spartan guest-house and a meal of granite-hard bacon and worm-riddled vegetables, served on a dirty tin plate and accompanied by a mug of lukewarm coffee. Just as we finished this unappetizing meal a messenger arrived to tell us that there had been a mistake and that a lavish lunch of turkey and Christmas pudding was waiting for us.

We listened spellbound to Mr Churchill who was at the top of his form. I asked the detective if the rumours of the P.M.'s illness had been exaggerated. 'Not at all,' he

GERALD PAWLE,
'Christmas with Churchill'
Blackwoods Magazine, December 1973

NEWSPAPERS THROUGHOUT THE ALLIED WORLD REPORTED **CHURCHILL'S pneumonia** with varying degrees of alarm, but by the final week before Christmas it seemed as if the worst had passed and the *News of the World* was able to run the headline 'Premier's Pneumonia Subsiding'. The irregularity of the premier's pulse appeared to be the cause of the greatest anxiety and the paper quoted a doctor as saying: 'This seems to indicate that the illness has thrown some strain on his heart. This could be partly accounted for by recent pressure of work lowering the patient's resistance at his age ... Mr Churchill must still be regarded as seriously ill.'

❄ ❄ ❄ ❄

KURT ZEHMISCH WAS A GERMAN SCHOOLTEACHER WHO FOUGHT IN THE trenches on the Western Front in the 134th Saxon Regiment. His war diaries were discovered in an attic near Leipzig in 1999. Below he describes the friendly exchanges that took place between the Germans and British over Christmas 1914. On Christmas Eve the shooting stopped and a few soldiers from each side emerged from the trenches, shook hands in no-man's-land and agreed not to shoot the following day:

Afterwards, we placed even more candles than before on our kilometre-long trench, as well as Christmas trees. It was the purest illumination — the British expressed their joy through whistles and clapping. Like most people, I spent the whole night awake. It was a wonderful, if somewhat cold night ... The English brought a soccer ball from the trenches, and pretty soon a lively game ensued. How marvellously wonderful, yet how strange it was. The English officers felt the same way about it. Thus Christmas, the celebration of Love, managed to bring mortal enemies together as friends for a time.

The British troops who fraternized with Zehmisch and his comrades were the men of the Royal Welch Fusiliers, the battalion of Robert Graves and Siegfried Sassoon. In his book *The War the Infantry Knew*, Captain J. Dunn, a medic in the Royal Welch, recorded how hostilities resumed on Boxing Day:

At 8.30 I fired three shots in the air and put up a flag with 'Merry Christmas' on it, and I climbed on the parapet. He put up a sheet with 'Thank you' on it, and the German Captain appeared on the parapet. We both bowed and saluted and got down into our respective trenches, and he fired two shots in the air, and the war was on again.

*1st day of Christmas Holidays. A sports programme was drawn
up and carried out during the next few days.*

*10:00 Gymkhana was started but postponed owing to rain
until 14:00 when it was successfully carried out.*

*18:00 Battalion Concert followed by a 'Beauty Competition'
was a well organised and appreciated entertainment.*

8TH ROYAL BERKSHIRE WAR DIARY, Monday, 23 December 1918, Beaurevoir, France

❊ ❊ ❊ ❊

THERE WAS NO RATIONING IN
Britain during Christmas
1939, the first year of the
Second World War. Public
morale was still high and
everyone spent freely in
the shops – partly because
rationing was planned to
start early in the New Year
and people were determined to **enjoy themselves while they could.**
The most popular gifts that year, not surprisingly, carried a military
theme or a practical purpose. Boys received figures of servicemen
in uniforms, and toy aircraft and tanks, while dolls of Red Cross
nurses were a popular choice for girls. Many grown-ups gave each
other steel helmets and fancy gas-mask cases. The following year it
was clear that the economic hardships of war had started to bite: the
most popular gift was soap.

❊ ❊ ❊ ❊

*'Peace Upon Earth!' was said. We sing it,
And pay a million priests to bring it.
After two thousand years of mass
We've got as far as poison gas.*

THOMAS HARDY (1840–1928), 'Christmas, 1924'

THE TURNING POINT OF THE AMERICAN War of Independence came on Christmas night 1776 when General George Washington, the future first president of the country, led what remained of his small demoralized army of patriots across the icy waters of the Delaware River. Just after dawn on Boxing Day, the American army of 2,400 soldiers **stormed the New Jersey town of Trenton**, quickly overwhelming the 1,500 German mercenary troops fighting for the British. (The Trenton troops, many of them still in bed, were said to be nursing hangovers from their Christmas Day celebrations.) As a military engagement, the battle was a non-event, but the date is regarded as

GEORGE·WASHINGTON

hugely significant in the destiny of the North American continent. The surprise attack brought the Americans their first victory in the war and boosted flagging morale across the anti-British communities of the colony after a series of major defeats, mainly in the New York area. One of the small handful of 'Patriots' seriously wounded in the skirmishes was an 18-year-old lieutenant called James Monroe, who in 1817 would become the fifth president of the United States. Monroe was hit in the shoulder by a musket ball and had lost great quantities of blood before a doctor clamped a severed artery, saving his life by a matter of minutes.

※ ※ ※ ※

Christmas Day No Firing. An unofficial armistice took place and troops of both sides met and buried the dead. The Battalion fixed up a board with 'A merry xmas' written on it in German midway between the trenches and was evidently much appreciated by the enemy.

2ND WILTSHIRE WAR DIARY, Friday, 25 December 1914, France

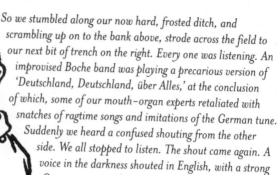

So we stumbled along our now hard, frosted ditch, and scrambling up on to the bank above, strode across the field to our next bit of trench on the right. Every one was listening. An improvised Boche band was playing a precarious version of 'Deutschland, Deutschland, über Alles,' at the conclusion of which, some of our mouth-organ experts retaliated with snatches of ragtime songs and imitations of the German tune. Suddenly we heard a confused shouting from the other side. We all stopped to listen. The shout came again. A voice in the darkness shouted in English, with a strong German accent, 'Come over here!' A ripple of mirth swept along our trench, followed by a rude outburst of mouth organs and laughter. Presently, in a lull, one of our sergeants repeated the request, 'Come over here!'

'You come half-way — I come half-way,' floated out of the darkness.

'Come on, then!' shouted the sergeant. 'I'm coming along the hedge!'

… After much suspicious shouting and jocular derision from both sides, our sergeant went along the hedge which ran at right-angles to the two lines of trenches. He was quickly out of sight; but, as we all listened in breathless silence, we soon heard a spasmodic conversation taking place out there in the darkness.

Presently, the sergeant returned. He had with him a few German cigars and cigarettes which he had exchanged for a couple of Machonochie's [tinned stew] *and a tin of Capstan* [tobacco]*, which he had taken with him. The séance was over, but it had given just the requisite touch to our Christmas Eve, something a little human and out of the ordinary routine.*

After months of vindictive sniping and shelling, this little episode came as an invigorating tonic, and a welcome relief to the daily monotony of antagonism. It did not lessen our ardour or determination; but just put a little human punctuation mark in our lives of cold and humid hate. Just on the right day, on Christmas Eve! But, as a curious episode, this was nothing in comparison to our experience on the following day.

On Christmas morning I awoke very early and emerged from my dug-out into the trench. It was a perfect day. A beautiful, cloudless blue sky. The ground hard and white, fading off towards the wood in a thin low-lying mist.

'Fancy all this hate, war, and discomfort on a day like this!' I thought to myself. The whole spirit of Christmas seemed to be there, so much so that I remember thinking, 'This indescribable something in the air, this Peace and Goodwill feeling, surely will have some effect on the situation here to-day!' And I wasn't far wrong …

…Walking about the trench a little later, discussing the curious affair of the night before, we suddenly became aware of the fact we were seeing a lot of evidences of Germans. Heads were bobbing about and showing over the parapet in a most reckless way, and, as we looked, this phenomenon became more and more pronounced.

A complete Boche figure suddenly appeared on the parapet, and looked about itself. This complaint became infectious. It didn't take 'Our Bert' [the British sergeant who exchanged goods with the Germans the previous day] long to be up on the skyline. This was the signal for more Boche anatomy to be disclosed, and this was replied to by our men, until in less time than it takes to tell, half a dozen or so of each of the belligerents were outside their trenches and were advancing towards each other in no-man's land.

I clambered up and over our parapet, and moved out across the field to look. Clad in a muddy suit of khaki and wearing a sheepskin coat and Balaclava helmet, I joined the throng about half-way across to the German trenches.

… Here they were — the actual practical soldiers of the German army. There was not an atom of hate on either side that day; and yet, on our side, not for a moment was the will to beat them relaxed. It was just like the interval between the rounds in a friendly boxing match. The difference in type between our men and theirs was very marked. There was no contrasting the spirit of the two parties. Our men, in their scratch costumes of dirty, muddy khaki, with their various assorted head-dresses of woollen helmets, mufflers and battered hats, were a light-hearted, open, humorous collection as opposed to the sombre demeanour and stolid appearance of the Huns in their grey-green faded uniforms, top boots, and pork-pie hats.

These devils, I could see, all wanted to be friendly; but none of them possessed the open, frank geniality of our men.

CAPTAIN BRUCE BAIRNSFATHER, ROYAL WARWICKSHIRE REGIMENT

from his book Bullets and Billets, 1916

Bairnsfather, who returned to England in 1915 after he was injured, became the best-known cartoonist of the Great War. He was sent back to the Front in the role of 'Officer Cartoonist' and his amusing illustrations were widely credited with helping to keep up the morale of the Commonwealth troops.

No better Christmas dinner was eaten that day in the whole United States. Invincible youth was around the board, and the two colonels lent dignity to the gathering, without detracting from its good cheer.

The table had been set late, and soon the winter twilight was approaching. As they took another slice of ham they heard the boom of a cannon on the far side of the Rappahannock. Harry went to the window and saw the white smoke rising from a point about three miles away.

'They can't be firing on us, can they, sir?' he said to Colonel Talbot. 'They wouldn't do it on a day like this.'

'No. There are two reasons. We're so far apart that it would be a waste of good powder and steel, and they would not violate Christmas in that manner. We and the Yankees have become too good friends for such outrageous conduct. If I may risk a surmise, I think it is merely a Christmas greeting.'

'I think so, too, sir. Listen, there goes a cannon on our side.'

… Then they listened, as the echo of the twelfth Southern shot died away on the stream, and no sound came after it. Twenty-four shots had been fired, twelve by each army, conveying Christmas good wishes, and the group in the house went back to their dinner. Some glasses had been found, and there was a thimbleful of wine, enough for everyone. The black cake was cut, and at a word from Colonel Talbot all rose and drank a toast to the mothers and wives and sweethearts and sisters they had left behind them.

Then the twilight thickened rapidly and the winter night came down upon them, hiding the ruined town, the blackened walls, the muddy streets and the icicles hanging from scorched timbers.

JOSEPH A. ALTSHELER
The Star of Gettysburg. 1915

The festival which we know as Christmas is above all the festival of peace and of the home. Among all free peoples the love of peace is profound, for this alone gives security to the home. But true peace is in the hearts of men, and it is the tragedy of this time that there are powerful countries whose whole direction and policy are based on aggression and the suppression of all that we hold dear for mankind. It is this that has stirred our peoples and given them a unity unknown in any previous war. We feel in our hearts that we are fighting against wickedness, and this conviction will give us strength from day to day to persevere until victory is assured.

… The men and women of our far-flung Empire working in their several vocations, with the one same purpose, all are members of the great Family of Nations which is prepared to sacrifice everything that freedom of spirit may be saved to the world.

Such is the spirit of the Empire; of the great Dominions, of India, of every Colony, large or small. From all alike have come offers of help, for which the Mother Country can never be sufficiently grateful. Such unity in aim and in effort has never been seen in the world before.

KING GEORGE VI, Christmas Day radio broadcast to the British Empire, 1939

❋ ❋ ❋ ❋

"**I wish** that every one of you could spend Christmas in Blighty." As that isn't possible I'll wish again—— that good friends at home will remember this Christmas to send out plenty of Waterman's Ideals. You deserve to have the Best.

Christmas Day. Work done on parapets. 'C' Coy in firing line and 'A' relieved 'D' Coy. Enemy very quiet as a whole. C.Q.M.S. Merritt was instantaneously killed whilst unloading rations from the trolley head by a Whiz bang [artillery shell].

6TH WILTSHIRE WAR DIARY, Saturday, 25 December 1915, France

XMAS 1916

"Many
of
'Em!"

I send you, my sailors and soldiers, hearty good wishes for Christmas and the New Year. My grateful thoughts are ever with you for victories gained, for hardships endured, and for your unfailing cheeriness. Another Christmas has come around, and we are still at war, but the Empire, confident in you, remains determined to win. May God bless you and protect you. At this Christmastide the Queen and I are thinking more than ever of the sick and wounded among my sailors and soldiers. From our hearts we wish them strength to bear their sufferings, speedy restoration to health, a peaceful Christmas and many happy years to come.

KING GEORGE V, Christmas message to his troops, 1916

❄ ❄ ❄ ❄

WOMAN'S WEEKLY, THE POPULAR MAGAZINE, CAME UP WITH A RAFT OF practical and inexpensive home-made gift and decoration suggestions for Christmas in December 1939. Gift ideas included *a dainty organdie* [stiff muslin] *lampshade … a necklace of flowers … an embroidered linen stamp book cover … a dressing table container for powdering pads … a crinoline lady tea cosy* [knitted] *… quickly knitted heelless bed socks …* An advertisement by retailers Henry Jones offered readers a series of *gay little purses* in the form of military headwear, with prices ranging from 2s 6d (+ 2d postage) for the cap of a humble 'bluejacket' sailor to 3s 6d for the more impressive headgear of an admiral or a field marshal.

The headquarter street we found swept and garnished, the flagstaff bedecked with holly, and a regimental band playing 'Home Sweet Home'. Dear old Sir Sam Browne did not believe in luxury when on campaign, but now for the first time I saw him at least comfortable … The mess anteroom was the camp street outside the dining tent; and at the fashionable late hour of eight we 'went in' to dinner, to the strains of the 'Roast Beef of Old England'. It was a right jovial feast, and the most cordial good fellowship prevailed. He would have been a cynical epicurean who would have criticised the appointments; the banquet itself was above all cavil. Rummaging among some old papers the other day, I found the menu, which deserves to be quoted: 'Soup — Julienne. Fish — Whitebait (from the Cabul River). Entrees — Cotelettes aux Champignons, Poulets a la Mayonnaise. Joints — Ham and fowls, roast beef, roast saddle of mutton, boiled brisket of beef, boiled leg of mutton and caper sauce. Curry — chicken. Sweets — Lemon jelly, blancmange, apricot tart, plum pudding. Grilled sardines, cheese fritters, cheese, dessert.' Truth compels the avowal that there was no table-linen, nor was the board resplendent with plate or gay with flowers. Table crockery was deficient, or to be more accurate, there was none. All the dishes were of metal, and the soup was eaten, or rather drunk, out of mugs and iron teacups. But it tasted none the worse on this account, and let it be recorded that there were champagne glasses, while between every two guests a portly magnum reared its golden head. Except 'The Queen', of course, there were but two toasts after the feast — one was 'Absent Friends', drunk in a wistful silence, and the other, the caterer's health, greeted with vociferous enthusiasm. A few fields off wood had been collecting all day for the Christmas camp-fire of the 10th Hussars, and by ten o'clock the blaze of it was mounting high into the murky gloom. A right merry and social gathering it was around the bright glow of this Yule log in a far-off land. The flames danced on the wide circle of bearded faces. On the tangled fleeces of the postheens, on the golden braid of the forage caps, on the sombre hoods of beshliks … The songs ranged from gay to grave; the former mood in the ascendancy … The bronzed troopers in the background shaded with their hands the fire-flash from their eyes; and as the familiar homely strain ceased that recalled home and love and trailed at the heart strings till the breast felt to heave and the tears to rise, there would be a little pause of eloquent silence which told how thoughts had gone astraying half across the globe to the loved ones in dear old England, and were loath to come back again to the rum and camp fire in Jellalabad plain. Ah, how many stood or sat around that camp fire that were never to see old England more?

ARCHIBALD FORBES (1838–1900)
English Illustrated Magazine, 1885

Forbes, a celebrated war correspondent and military historian, describes a Christmas Day spent with General Sam Browne's troops in a camp outside Jalalabad, during the Second Afghan War.

Dear Eq, I have received your letter & Christmas card for which many thanks. You seem to be having a toffee time for a soldier, what with your Christmas cards & your straw mattresses & 3 blankets — 3 blankets! Think of your old pal sleeping on a waterproof sheet laid on cold wet clay, with all his clothes and overcoat on — both of which are sodden with clay — and covered with a soaking wet blanket. It's an absolute fact that when we come out of the trenches I, with the help of another, wrung the water out of my blanket and overcoat, when dry stood up by itself! Still while I may envy you, I do not grudge you your comfort. Be as comfortable as you can while you can … We were in the trenches again for three days before and on Christmas Day and were relieved on Boxing morning … We had decided to give the Germans a Christmas present of 3 carols and 5 rounds rapid. Accordingly as soon as night fell we started & the strains of 'While Shepherds' (beautifully rendered by the choir) arose upon the air. We finished that and paused preparatory to giving the 2nd item on the programme. But lo! We heard answering strains arising from their lines. Also they started shouting across to us. Therefore we stopped any hostile operations and commenced to shout back. One of them shouted 'A Merry Christmas English. We're not shooting tonight'. We yelled back a similar message & from that time until we were relieved on Boxing morning @ 4am not a shot was fired. After this shouting had gone on for some time they stuck up a light. Not to be outdone, so did we. Then up went another. So we shoved up another. Soon the two lines looked like an illuminated fete … Next morning, Christmas Day, they started getting out of the trenches & waving & some came towards us. We went out and met them & had the curious pleasure of chatting with the men who had been doing their best to kill us, and we them. I exchanged a cigarette for a cigar with one of them (Not a bad exchange eh?) & as some of them spoke English had quite a long conversation. One fellow said that as soon as the war was over he was 'going back to England by express.' He had a wife and 2 children in the Alexander Rd!!

PTE ERNEST MORLEY, 1/16th Londons, diary entry, 29 December 1914,

'Somewhere in France'

❄ ❄ ❄ ❄

Threatened Coal Famine

A North Country correspondent writes: One of the most unsatisfactory prospects of the New Year's trade is the impending famine in coal. This has been brought about by a variety of causes which can

be traced to influences altogether outside of commercial or industrial operations. The demand for coal is probably greater than it has ever been known to be, but the supply, instead of increasing, is falling off. One reason for this position is to be found in the fact that colliers are earning more money and will not work full time. A second reason is found in the withdrawal of many reservists for the [Boer] war who up until recently were employed in the coal pits, and a still further reason is to be traced to the calling out of the militia. The collieries in the country are consequently not so briskly worked as of late and the colliers are taking a longer holiday at Christmas and the New Year than usual.

Daily News, 26 December 1899

GNEISENAU
SCHARNHORST.

ON BOXING DAY 1943, BRITAIN INFLICTED A SIGNIFICANT BLOW ON the German fleet when Royal Navy ships sank the German battle cruiser *Scharnhorst* in the Arctic. Together with its equally formidable sister ship the *Gneisenau* (they were known to the British as the 'ugly sisters'), the *Scharnhorst* had caused major disruption to the convoys bringing vital supplies to Britain and Russia from the United States. Enigma, the British code-breaking machine decoded German naval signals, revealing that the *Scharnhorst*, which had recently sunk the British cruiser *Rawalpindi*, was on its way to attack an Anglo-American convoy to Russia. In what became known as the Battle of the North Cape, the 31,000-ton battle cruiser was surprised by the British battleship *Duke of York* and a number of cruisers. After a day-long chase and battle, the giant *Scharnhorst* sank to the ocean's floor with the loss of almost 2,000 men. Only 36 survived. That night Admiral Bruce Fraser on board the *Duke of York* urged his officers: 'Gentlemen, the battle against *Scharnhorst* has ended in victory for us. I hope that if any of you are ever called upon to lead a ship into action against an opponent many times superior, you will command your ship as gallantly as *Scharnhorst* was commanded today.'

BLIGHTY CHRISTMAS NUMBER, 1917.

Sandy : "LEND ME A FRANC, TAM."
Tam : "NA, I CANNA DAE THAT."
Sandy : "IT'S A SMA' THING TO REFUSE."
Tam : "AY, BUT YOU WOULDNAE PAY ME BACK, AND THEN YOU AN' ME WAD QUARREL ; SO WE MAY JUST
AS WEEL QUARREL NOO, WHILE THE MONEY'S IN MY POCKET."

Horace Gaffron.

I think I have seen one of the most extraordinary sights today that anyone has ever seen. About 10 o'clock this morning I was peeping over the parapet when I saw a German, waving his arms, and presently two of them got out of their trenches and some came towards ours. We were just going to fire on them when we saw they had no rifles so one of our men went out to meet them and in about two minutes the ground between the two lines of trenches was swarming with men and officers of both sides, shaking hands and wishing each other a happy Christmas.

SECOND LIEUTENANT DOUGAN CHATER, 2nd Gordon Highlanders, in a letter to his
mother from a trench near Armentières, Christmas Day 1914

Practically every man was occupied in cleaning trenches and repairing landslides. Communications trenches were bad ... The front line had a good deal of water in places, pumps were set to work and certain progress made ... Enemy was very quiet except for a few minenwerfers [mine launchers] about BOYAU 16 and an occasional rifle grenade, neither of which did any damage.

... Strict orders were issued against fraternising with the enemy on Christmas Day, men were warned they would be tried by FGCM for any attempt on their part to constitute a truce, and orders were given that Germans showing themselves would be fired on. During the day our heavy and other artillery bombarded heavily AUCHY LEZ LA BASSEE and the German front and second line with reported good results.

1ST ROYAL BERKSHIRE WAR DIARY, FRIDAY, 24 DECEMBER 1915, FRANCE

❄ ❄ ❄ ❄

We had a white Xmas here and it began to snow on Xmas eve, and we had about six weeks of it. It kept on freezing day and night all the time, and were snowed up and frozen up then, but we had our happy Xmas Day on New Years Day after coming out.

Our Christmas dinner in the line or shell holes was composed of tins of bully beef and a few hard biscuits thrown into a canteen, with a big handful of snow to make water. We could make some Bully Stew for dinner that day and we enjoyed it fine, as there was nothing else to have at that time. Snow the only thing to make water as we couldn't use the water in our bottles we carried for it. It was a crime then which would have won us 14 days pay stopped, and we didn't want that now.

The ground was covered in snow and the water in the shell holes was frozen. We were not supposed to use it or drink it at any time. We had to be very careful about lighting a fire because of the smoke in the daytime and the light of the fire at night as well. If Jerry had seen it we may have had a gentle visitor come over to visit us and wish us a Happy Xmas and a Xmas box to wish us a happy New Year all in one day ...

We had our real Christmas dinner on New Years day better late than never. We had a whole pig for a company of men, and also Xmas pudding which came up to us in tins, and so much beer for each man and cigs and a good concert at night. Some of the men got drunk and drowned their joys and sorrows in beer and some sang them away. It was blinking cold for us. A few days later Jerry came over and dropped a few hard boiled eggs, or bombs close by our camp, on some transport lines and laid out a number of men for us, just to wish us all a happy new year.

PTE ALFRED LEWIS, 6th Northamptons, 1917

The nation has made a resolve that war or no war, the children of England will not be cheated out of the one day they look forward to all year. So, as far as possible, this will be an old-fashioned Christmas, at least for the children.

MINISTRY OF INFORMATION FILM
Christmas under Fire, 1941

❄ ❄ ❄ ❄

CHRISTMAS DAY 1941, ONE OF THE DARKEST MOMENTS IN THE history of the British Empire, is known as Black Christmas in Hong Kong. This was the day that the hopelessly outnumbered British garrison surrendered the Crown Colony to the Japanese, marking the beginning of a brutal occupation that cost the lives of tens of thousands of POWS and civilians. The Japanese began their attack on 8 December, and mounted a land invasion 10 days later, rounding up captured soldiers and bayoneting them to death. The Japanese bombed water mains supplying the city, and took control of the reservoirs and the power stations. At 3.30 in the afternoon on Christmas Day, the Governor of Hong Kong, Sir Mark Aitchison Young, surrendered in person to Japanese generals at their headquarters in the Peninsula Hong Kong Hotel. It was the first time that a British colony had surrendered to an invading force. The 6,500 men of the 10,000-strong garrison who survived the invasion battles were transported to prisoner-of-war camps, where it is estimated over half of them perished in appalling conditions.

❄ ❄ ❄ ❄

AT THE START OF THE SECOND BOER WAR IN 1899, BEFORE SIGNIFICANT reinforcements had arrived in the Cape, the British suffered a number of military setbacks that horrified the public back home. In the week before Christmas, known as 'Black Week', the British suffered heavy casualties and the towns of Mafeking and Ladysmith

were besieged by marauding Boer forces
who swarmed over the borders from their
traditional homelands. The situation was so
grave that Queen Victoria, now in her 81st
year, broke with tradition and remained at
Windsor Castle to host a Christmas Day tea
for the wives and families of soldiers serving
in southern Africa. The following day she
wrote in her diary:

All the women and children trooped in, and after looking at the tree they all sat down to tea at two very long tables, below the tree. Everyone helped to serve them, including my family, old and young, and my ladies and gentlemen.

I was rolled up and down round the tables, after which I went away for a short while to have my own tea, returning when the tree was beginning to be stripped, handing myself many of the things to the wives and dear little children … there were some babies of a few weeks and months old … It was a very touching sight, when one thinks of the poor husbands and fathers, who are all away, and some of whom may not return. They seemed all very much pleased.

❄ ❄ ❄ ❄

IN THEIR CHRISTMAS-WEEK ISSUE OF 1939, *WOMAN'S WEEKLY* ENCOURAGED housewives to cheer up their anti-shatter blackout blinds, insisting:

There is no reason why the precaution of pasting strips of paper on our windows should make them look so depressingly ugly. With a little ingenuity they can be extremely attractive for Christmas time … Use black paper cut into three-quarter inch strips which, when posted diagonally, will give the effect of leaded diamond panes. Then find a pretty wall paper border, cut it out, and paste it all around the edge of the window … You will be surprised what a difference this makes to your room.

❄ ❄ ❄ ❄

Of course you're doing some entertaining this Christmas, not just for your family and lifelong friends, but for some of our new friends from across the Atlantic. I know you won't let food restrictions deter you from offering hospitality you will all enjoy so much. After all, it seems only right that some of the lease-and-lend* *foods should be used for this purpose. What shall we give the American boys to make them feel at home? Try some typical American dishes. You're going to like them so much that they are certain to become part of English menus from now on.*

If tea is the meal you can best manage, it would be hard to beat … Apple Sauce Cake … Peanut Cookies, Spiced Pork and Cabbage and Baking Powder Biscuits.

Woman's Pictorial magazine, 19 December 1942

*Supplies to Europe from America under lease-and-lend agreement.

It was Christmas '44 and we were obviously looking round for a Christmas dinner. Although turkeys in that part of Italy at that time were very plentiful, it seemed to be that every place we got to and wanted a turkey, the Canadians had got there first. And they had more or less cleared the place of turkeys for their Christmas. So we thought 'I don't know, we're going to be without a Christmas dinner' and somebody suggested that one or two nights before we'd come through a farm, a big farm, where there were a lot of pigs. We decided to go back to this farm and see what we could get. This was at night-time. We took the truck back to this farm and we came away with a little pig. The only way we could get this pig away ... — and this may sound terrible — the only way to stop it grunting was to stick your fingers up its nostrils so it couldn't make a noise. And somebody knew how to do this apparently — and this was done. So we got it in the back of the truck and going back we had to go back through a road patrol, which was manned by MPs [Military Police]. So of course we were very undecided how we were going to get the pig through the patrol. So we covered the pig over in the back of the truck, hence the two fingers up his nostrils to keep him quiet, and somehow or other we got through the patrol. The thing was — where to keep the pig? Where we were billeted were like flats with verandas and we got this pig up into one of the flats and we just blocked it in and let it loose on the veranda. Well, that was all right until the CO came out in the morning and looked up and saw the pig running around. He wants to know who's responsible and of course we owned up. I said I was one of them.

He [the CO] was what we used to call 'one of the boys' — although he was a Major he was a very nice fellow — and I said 'Well look, it's obvious we're

going to be stuck here for Christmas and the lads of course had no Christmas dinner. So we decided to go out and get some.' So his words were: 'You can't keep the bloody thing up there forever, so you've got to find somewhere for it to go' ... Anyway, to cut a long story short — on the day before Christmas we had to approach the cook staff to kill the pig and cook it. So this was agreed upon, providing the Officers' Mess had a leg — so we agreed to this — we had to. So of course the pig was killed and roast and cooked and a happy ending to a Christmas — except for the pig!

JOHN ALBERT LUXFORD, NCO,
1st Bn King's Royal Rifle Corps (IWM archives)

❊ ❊ ❊ ❊

THE FINAL CHRISTMAS OF THE SECOND WORLD WAR WAS PROBABLY the most difficult. Worn down by six years of conflict, bereavement and increasing deprivation, the British people's hopes that the war would be over by the end of 1944 were dashed by events on the front. Three dozen V1 and V2 Doodlebug missiles struck towns and cities in northern England, reminding people that though Germany was on the retreat, technology still allowed her to strike deep into enemy territory. Many cities had almost completely run out of alcohol, which only compounded the sense of gloom. There was some good news, though, with the relaxation of blackout laws, which allowed people to **illuminate their homes** for the first time since the war began. The Ministry of Food also increased rations of sweets, sugar and meat, but the general hardship is reflected in the issuing of instructions on how people might decorate their homes ... with vegetables.

THE SERVICEMAN

I WAS A FEW MONTHS INTO MY FIRST TOUR OF NORTHERN IRELAND, which perhaps explains why I was chosen to work the Christmas Day shift, alongside 'Mongo', another Navy pilot, in one of the squadron's Sea Kings. From late evening through to the small hours of Boxing Day, we were scheduled to carry out a whole variety of tasks across South Armagh: moving troops, supporting the police and transporting supplies and equipment between the many army bases and outposts strung out across 'bandit country'. It was just another routine mission in Ulster, but flying at night and at low-level is as demanding and challenging as helicopter flying gets, even without terrorists taking pot shots at you.

We were based at Aldergrove airbase next to Belfast International airport, and it was from there that Mongo and I prepared to set off in the afternoon of Christmas Day. The rest of the lads were taking the mickey out of us as they settled down in the Runway Club, the makeshift officers' mess where we used to congregate for a few beers. We couldn't go out much in Belfast, for obvious security reasons, so most of our entertaining and drinking was done in that little prefab hut. When some of us had gone into the city centre for a night out a few weeks earlier, it had almost ended in disaster. We were happily chatting to some local girls when one of the boys let slip that he had spent the day working in 'bandit country'. The girls immediately twigged who we were, put down their drinks and turned on their stiletto heels. They walked straight over to a group of heavy-looking lads at the bar and started pointing at us. All military personnel in Northern Ireland are under the strictest orders not to get into trouble with the locals and so, abandoning our pints where they stood, we took off as fast as we could. We all scarpered in different directions before making our separate ways back to our car. When we got there we realized that Midge – a young guy also on his first tour of the province – was missing. We were beginning to fear the worst when we heard a muffled noise coming from the boot. It was Midge. He thought it the safest place to wait until the rest of us arrived!

As the lads put on their paper hats and settled down to their turkey dinner, Mongo and I put on our helmets and night-vision goggles (NVGs) and lifted off into the rapidly fading light. It was pitch dark by the time we came in to land at the heavily fortified military base at Bessbrook, a huge old cotton mill in a staunchly republican area from where we supplied other military outposts. Going by road was not an option in the heart of bandit country. Everything was done by helicopter. It's a forbidding place, Bessbrook Mill, a bit like a high-security prison with its miles of barbed wire strung over the towering red-brick walls and corrugated-iron roofs. When we arrived and relieved the RAF crew, there was a boisterous atmosphere inside as the other soldiers and aviators were tucking into their Christmas dinners and generally getting into the festive spirit.

Mongo and I, the only aircrew working in South Armagh that evening, were getting a bit fed up with all this partying. You don't get many opportunities to let your hair down out in Ulster and we wanted a bit of the fun too, so our plan was to carry out our tasks as quick as possible and get back to Bessbrook a bit earlier than scheduled. But my heart sank when we went to pick up the timetable from Buzzard, the air transport co-ordinator, and realized that there was masses to do – thanks to our chums in the RAF, who had obviously dawdled on their shift and left us a backlog of tasks to clear. 'RAF bastards!' we muttered in unison. As we headed out to the helicopter to start our shift, all the other pilots blew out their streamers at us and gave us a rude rendition of 'Rudolph the Red-Nosed Reindeer'.

We tried to execute our tasks as promptly and efficiently as possible, without taking any risks. Dozens of troops needed inserting and picking up from various locations across the county; we picked up a suspect arrested by the RUC; another RUC officer needed to be flown back to base for medical attention after slashing his leg open while pursuing a suspect. Flying at night is tiring at the best of times because you really have to concentrate with the NVGs on, especially when you are so low to the ground. It was perhaps fitting then that to cap a hard, crappy night's work we finished the shift by transporting a two-ton tub of soldier shit from one of the watchtowers back to base from where it could be taken away to be treated. It was five in the morning and the Christmas party was long finished by the time we finally crawled into our sleeping bags, exhausted and pissed off. 'Well, happy bloody Christmas, bud!' I said to Mongo as I turned off the light by my bunk. There was a pause and then, out of the darkness, came the sound of a rather flat Christmas streamer being blown.

LT CDR JONJO JOHNSON, Fleet Air Arm

Happy Reunions, Terrible Tantrums:

Christmas and the Family

At Christmas little children sing and merry bells jingle
The cold winter air makes our hands and faces tingle
And happy families go to church and cheerily they mingle
And the whole business is unbelievably dreadful, if you're single.

WENDY COPE, 'A Christmas Poem'

Christmas time! That man must be a misanthrope indeed, in whose breast something like a jovial feeling is not roused — in whose mind some pleasant associations are not awakened — by the recurrence of Christmas. There are people who will tell you that Christmas is not to them what it used to be; that each succeeding Christmas has found some cherished hope, or happy prospect, of the year before, dimmed or passed away; that the present only serves to remind them of reduced circumstances and straitened incomes — of the feasts they once bestowed on hollow friends, and of the cold looks that meet them now, in adversity and misfortune. Never heed such dismal reminiscences. There are few men

who have lived long enough in the world, who cannot call up such thoughts any day in the year. Then do not select the merriest of the three hundred and sixty-five for your doleful recollections, but draw your chair nearer the blazing fire — fill the glass and send round the song — and if your room be smaller than it was a dozen years ago, or if your glass be filled with reeking punch, instead of sparkling wine, put a good face on the matter, and empty it off-hand, and fill another, and troll off the old ditty you used to sing, and thank God it's no worse. Look on the merry faces of your children (if you have any) as they sit round the fire. One little seat may be empty; one slight form that gladdened the father's heart, and roused the mother's pride to look upon, may not be there. Dwell not upon the past; think not that one short year ago, the fair child now resolving into dust, sat before you, with the bloom of health upon its cheek, and the gaiety of infancy in its joyous eye. Reflect upon your present blessings — of which every man has many — not on your past misfortunes, of which all men have some. Fill your glass again, with a merry face and contented heart. Our life on it, but your Christmas shall be merry, and your new year a happy one!

Who can be insensible to the outpourings of good feeling, and the honest interchange of affectionate attachment, which abound at this season of the year? A Christmas family-party! We know nothing in nature more delightful! There seems a magic in the very name of Christmas. Petty jealousies and discords are forgotten; social feelings are awakened, in bosoms to which they have long been strangers; father and son, or brother and sister, who have met and passed with averted gaze, or a look of cold recognition, for months before, proffer and return the cordial embrace, and bury their past animosities in their present happiness. Kindly hearts that have yearned towards each other, but have been withheld by false notions of pride and self-dignity, are again reunited, and all is kindness and benevolence! Would that Christmas lasted the whole year through (as it ought), and that the prejudices and passions which deform our better nature, were never called into action among those to whom they should ever be strangers!

The Christmas family-party that we mean, is not a mere assemblage of relations, got up at a week or two's notice, originating this year, having no family precedent in the last, and not likely to be repeated in the next. No. It is an annual gathering of all the accessible members of the family, young or old, rich or poor; and all the children look forward to it, for two months beforehand, in a fever of anticipation...

CHARLES DICKENS

Sketches by Boz: 'A Christmas Dinner'

135

10 Christmas-time survival tips from Parentline Plus

1. Get together and write a list of what everyone wants to do. Decide what is really important, and if possible prioritize.
2. Make a list of who needs to see who. Particularly important with extended stepfamilies.
3. Use a calendar. Make a note of which family members are doing what and when.
4. Schedule in some time to recharge your own batteries. If you're well rested you'll be able to enjoy your family more.
5. Don't try to do everything yourself. Make a list of jobs which need to be done and allocate them between the whole family.
6. Don't try and keep everyone happy all the time. You'll collapse under the pressure.
7. If this is your first Christmas as a stepfamily, your child may feel confused and maybe even angry. Try to allocate some time that you can spend alone together to reassure them that your love for them has not changed.
8. Adults don't have to enjoy being with children all the time. Allow some time for you to be alone with your partner, other family members or friends.
9. Don't assume that everyone else is having a wonderful time. Everyone else is muddling through just like you, so try not to put pressure on yourself.
10. Don't act in anger. If everything gets too much, remove yourself from the situation and perhaps call a friend or relative.

The Little Strangs say the 'good words' as they call them, before going to bed, aloud and at their father's knee, or rather in the pit of his stomach. One of them was lately heard to say 'Forgive us our Christmases, as we forgive them that Christmas against us.'

SAMUEL BUTLER, English writer, c. 1890

Daily Mail reporter: What would you give your worst enemy for Christmas?
Viscount Linley: Dinner with Princess Michael!

I was nine or ten years old when my father was sacked on Christmas Day. He was a manager, the results had not been good, he lost a game on December 22nd or 23rd. On Christmas Day, the telephone rang and he was sacked in the middle of our lunch.

JOSÉ MOURINHO, football manager

❅ ❅ ❅ ❅

THERE ARE CHRISTMAS ROWS, AND THERE ARE CHRISTMAS ROWS. ON 25 December 1929, North Carolina tobacco farmer Charlie Lawson, a hitherto respected local figure, went into a **murderous frenzy**, slaying his wife and six of their seven children before taking his own life. The murders inspired poems and songs, the most famous being 'The Ballad of Charlie Lawson'. The motives behind the mass murder remain a mystery, but police are refusing to rule out the possibility that Mr Lawson may have lost at Scrabble.

❅ ❅ ❅ ❅

After three days guests and fish stink.

JEWISH SAYING

Three current England **test cricketers** were born on Christmas Day: opening batsmen Marcus Trescothick (1975) and Alistair Cook (1984) and fast bowler Simon Jones (1978).

✳ ✳ ✳ ✳

December 24 — I am a poor man, but I would gladly give ten shillings to find out who sent me the insulting Christmas card I received this morning. I never insult people; why should they insult me? The worst part of the transaction is, that I find myself suspecting all my friends …

Christmas Day — We caught the 10.20 train at Paddington, and spent a pleasant day at Carrie's mother's. The country was quite nice and pleasant, although the roads were sloppy. We dined in the middle of the day, just ten of us, and talked over old times. If everybody had a nice, uninterfering mother-in-law, such as I have, what a deal of happiness there would be in the world. Being all in good spirits, I proposed her health, and I made, I think, a very good speech.

I concluded, rather neatly, by saying: 'On an occasion like this — whether relatives, friends, or acquaintances — we are all inspired with good feelings towards each other. We are of one mind, and think only of love and friendship. Those who have quarrelled with absent friends should kiss and make it up. Those who happily have not fallen out, can kiss all the same.'

I saw the tears in the eyes of both Carrie and her mother, and must say I felt very flattered by the compliment. That dear old Reverend John Panzy Smith, who married us, made a most cheerful and amusing speech, and said he should act on my suggestion respecting the kissing. He then walked round the table and kissed all the ladies, including Carrie. Of course one did not object to this; but I was more than staggered when a young fellow named Moss, who was a stranger to me, and who had scarcely spoken a word through dinner, jumped up suddenly with a sprig of mistletoe, and exclaimed: 'Hulloh! I don't see why I shouldn't be in on this scene.' Before one could realise what he was about to do, he kissed Carrie and the rest of the ladies.

Fortunately the matter was treated as a joke, and we all laughed; but it was a dangerous experiment, and I felt very uneasy for a moment as to the result. I subsequently referred to the matter to Carrie, but she said: 'Oh, he's not much more than a boy.' I said that he had a very large moustache for a boy. Carrie replied: 'I didn't say he was not a nice boy.'

George and Weedon Grossmith
The Diary of a Nobody, **1892**

IN THE 1840S ILLUSTRATIONS OF THE ROYAL family gathered around a heavily decorated Christmas tree appeared in the popular newspaper the *Illustrated London News*. In the years following, it became *de rigueur* for well-to-do households up and down the land to have a tree of their own in the home. It is difficult to overstate the moral and cultural influence the royal family held over the British public in Victoria's reign. 'If it was good enough for Victoria and Albert, then it'll certainly do for us' was the prevailing attitude of the ever-expanding middle classes. Victoria's example, combined with the popularity of Dickens's Christmas tales, entrenched the notion of Christmas as a happy family event in people's minds.

IT IS CLEAR FROM VICTORIA'S DIARIES THAT LONG before Prince Albert turned up at Windsor Castle clutching his Norway spruce, a box of baubles and a string of candied almonds, the family Christmas was already well established in the royal household. On Christmas Eve 1832, the 13-year-old princess noted in her diary:

After dinner ... we then went into the drawing-room near the dining-room ... There were two large round tables on which were placed two trees hung with lights and sugar ornaments. All the presents being placed round the trees ... Mamma gave me a little lovely pink bag which she had worked with a little sachet likewise done by her; a beautiful little opal brooch and earrings, books, some lovely prints, a pink satin dress and a cloak lined with fur. Aunt Sophia gave me a dress which she worked herself, and Aunt Mary a pair of amethyst earrings ... We then went to my room where I had arranged Mamma's table.

I gave Mamma a white bag which I had worked, a collar and a steel chain for Flora; Aunt Sophia a pair of turquoise earrings; Lehzen [her governess] a little white and gold pincushion and a pin with two little gold hearts hanging to it ... Mamma then took me up into my bedroom with all the ladies. There was my new toilet table with a white muslin cover over pink, and all my silver things standing on it with a fine new looking-glass. I stayed up until half past nine.

It was in this winter that his attention was particularly drawn to the festival of Christmas, which, apparently, he had scarcely noticed in London. On the subject of all feasts of the Church he held views of an almost grotesque peculiarity. He looked upon each of them as nugatory and worthless, but the keeping of Christmas appeared to him by far the most hateful, and nothing less than an act of idolatry. 'The very word is Popish', he used to exclaim, 'Christ's Mass!' pursing up his lips with the gesture of one who tastes asafoetida by accident. Then he would adduce the antiquity of the so-called feast, adapted from horrible heathen rites, and itself a soiled relic of the abominable Yule-Tide. He would denounce the horrors of Christmas until it almost made me blush to look at a holly-berry. On Christmas Day of this year 1857 our villa saw a very unusual sight. My father had given strictest charge that no difference whatever was to be made in our meals on that day; the dinner was to be neither more copious than usual nor less so. He was obeyed, but the servants, secretly rebellious, made a small plum-pudding for themselves. (I discovered afterwards, with pain, that Miss Marks received a slice of it in her boudoir.) Early in the afternoon, the maids — of whom we were now advanced to keeping two — kindly remarked that 'the poor dear child ought to have a bit, anyhow', and wheedled me into the kitchen, where I ate a slice of plum-pudding. Shortly I began to feel that pain inside which in my frail state was inevitable, and my conscience smote me violently. At length I could bear my spiritual anguish no longer, and bursting into the study I called out: 'Oh! Papa, Papa, I have eaten of flesh offered to idols!' It took some time, between my sobs, to explain what had happened. Then my father sternly said: 'Where is the accursed thing?' I explained that as much as was left of it was still on the kitchen table. He took me by the hand, and ran with me into the midst of the startled servants, seized what remained of the pudding, and with the plate in one hand and me still tight in the other, ran until we reached the dust-heap, when he flung the idolatrous confectionery on to the middle of the ashes, and then raked it deep down into the mass. The suddenness, the violence, the velocity of this extraordinary act made an impression on my memory which nothing will ever efface.

EDMUND GOSSE (1849–1928), English writer
Father and Son

✻ ✻ ✻ ✻

TWELFTH NIGHT WAS AN IMPORTANT EVENT FOR QUEEN VICTORIA and her family as the royal household brought the Christmas celebrations to a joyful, if mildly alarming, conclusion. Each year, a short play was staged by her children and a special Twelfth Night cake was served. The family also settled down to a musical recital of some sort; very often it was a piece by Felix Mendelssohn, her favourite contemporary composer. **Parlour games** were a feature of the day too and the family favourite was an entertainment by which they all tried to grab raisins from a bowl of flaming brandy. The last person to go threw salt into the bowl to produce a bright yellow flame. Strip those Victorians of their whalebone corsets and waxed moustaches for the day, and golly, they knew how to party.

❄ ❄ ❄ ❄

Christmas Day 1946: Drove to Midnight Mass at Nympsfield very slowly on frozen roads with Teresa, Bron [Auberon] and Vera [nursery maid] in the back of the car. The little church was so painfully crowded. We sat behind a dozen insubordinate little boys who coughed and stole and wrangled. The chairs were packed so tight it was impossible to kneel straight. Drove home very slowly and did not get to bed until 2.30am ... I made a fair show of geniality throughout the day though the spectacle of a litter of shoddy toys and half-eaten sweets sickened me. Everything is so badly made nowadays that none of the children's presents seemed to work. Luncheon was cold and poorly cooked. A ghastly day.

EVELYN WAUGH (1903–66),
English writer
Diaries

For Boxing Day, Grandma Osborne had perfected a pumpkin trick which turned all the cold Christmas pudding and mince pies suddenly into funeral baked meats. She did it almost on the stroke of five and in one wand-like incantation. Lying back in the Hymnal position, she would close her eyes, smile her thin gruel of a smile and say, 'Ah well, there's another Christmas over.' I dreaded the supreme satisfaction with which she laid the body of Christmas to rest. In one phrase she crushed the festive flower and the jubilant heart.

JOHN OSBORNE (1929–94), English playwright, *A Better Class of Person*

❊ ❊ ❊ ❊

Each Christmas, at this time, my beloved father broadcast a message to his people in all parts of the world ... As he used to do, I am speaking to you from my own home, where I am spending Christmas with my family ... My father and my grandfather before him, worked hard all their lives to unite our peoples ever more closely, and to maintain its ideals which were so near to their hearts. I shall strive to carry on their work.

EXTRACT FROM QUEEN ELIZABETH II's FIRST CHRISTMAS MESSAGE, 1952

We had a delightful Christmas yesterday — just such a Christmas thirty or forty years ago we used to have under Father's and Mother's supervision in 20th street and 57th street. At seven all the children came in to open the big, bulgy stockings in our bed; Kermit's terrier, Allan, a most friendly little dog, adding to the children's delight by occupying the middle of the bed. From Alice to Quentin, each child was absorbed in his or her stocking, and Edith certainly managed to get the most wonderful stocking toys. Bob was in looking on, and Aunt Emily, of course. Then, after breakfast, we all formed up and went into the library, where bigger toys were on separate tables for the children. I wonder whether there ever can come in life a thrill of greater exaltation and rapture than that which comes to one between the ages of say six and fourteen, when the library door is thrown open and you walk in to see all the gifts, like a materialized fairy land, arrayed on your special table?

US PRESIDENT THEODORE ROOSEVELT,
letter to his sister, Mrs Douglas Robinson, 26 December 1903

❄ ❄ ❄ ❄

Every year on Christmas day I like to tell my mother that I'm a lesbian, even though I'm not. It just gets everything going.

JENNY ECLAIR (1960–), comedian

---

10 great family films for grown-ups at Christmas

It's a Wonderful Life
A Christmas Carol
Miracle on 34th Street
Trading Places
White Christmas
The Bishop's Wife

Christmas in Connecticut
Scrooged
National Lampoon's
    Christmas Vacation
Christmas with the Kranks

---

10 great family films for kids at Christmas

The Snowman
A Christmas Story
How the Grinch Stole
    Christmas
Gremlins
A Charlie Brown Christmas
A Christmas Carol

The Muppet Christmas
    Carol
Prancer
Rudolph the Red-Nosed
    Reindeer (1964 TV
    version)
Home Alone

THE DISC JOCKEY

I'VE WORKED ON CHRISTMAS DAY FOR MOST OF MY ADULT LIFE AND IT'S
only recently, since I had my children, that I've been at home for
the entire day. Working at Christmas never used to bother me when
I was younger. In fact, I jumped at the chance of getting away from
the tension that tends to build up at home as the day goes on and
the relatives pour in the door. Christmas was the high season for
arguments in our house!

With a job in television or radio, you soon get accustomed to
working unsociable hours. Over the years, I grew used to slipping
into the house in the small hours of Boxing Day morning, and
quietly making myself a cold turkey sandwich before slipping up
to my bedroom. Inevitably, the sideboards would be covered in all
the washed-up plates and dishes and I'd feel quietly pleased that,
once again, I had managed to escape the Christmas mayhem and the
marathon post-meal clear-up.

The one time I didn't feel like working on Christmas Day was in
1986, the year I got married. Missing Christmas is no great sacrifice
when you're single, but that year I really wanted to be snuggled
up with my husband. I was working as a vision mixer for GMTV
in those days and there was no chance of getting the day off. That
particular Christmas Day was also memorable because the producers
took the slightly risky decision to squeeze every single person in
the building into the final shot of the programme. The entire
production crew plus the cleaners, security guards, the bloke in the
coffee shop round the corner – anyone who happened to be in the
vicinity – all dropped what they were doing, and came on to the set
and surrounded Anne Diamond and Nick Owen on the sofas. Once
the crowd had assembled, the cameramen set their cameras to wide
angle, locked them off and ran round to join us. It was a fantastically
chaotic scene as everyone jostled into the picture, laughing and
waving. It felt a little nerve-racking knowing that we were going live
to the nation and there wasn't a single human being at the controls!

I've spent most of my working life as a DJ for Radio One, Radio
Two, Virgin and recently Smooth Radio and I've probably done
as many Christmas Day shows as any living DJ. I used to love
walking into Broadcasting House, just north of Oxford Circus,
on Christmas Day. The commissionaires (receptionists to you and
me) at the main entrance to the building are well known for their

serious approach to their job but on Christmas Day even these professional custodians in their military-style uniforms ditched their customary reserve and waved us through with a grin and a festive greeting.

The streets outside were also unrecognizable from a normal day. All but a handful of shops, cafés and pubs were shut, there were no crowds, and anyone who happened to be out and about seemed to be in a generous mood, dispensing greetings to whoever was sharing the pavement with them. In that one day I used to exchange more nods and hellos with strangers than I would for the rest of the year. It was as if everyone had decided to take the day off being grumpy or suspicious. The next day they'd be barging you out of the way or telling you to get lost, but on Christmas Day it's all smiles and greetings. That's what I love about Christmas — the goodwill of strangers.

There is one Christmas Day broadcast I'll never forget. I was doing the morning show on Radio Two for Terry Wogan and I was talking live on air when the studio door opened and in walked a vicar ... wearing an enormous amount of make-up! He had come in to do the 'Pause for Thought' slot, in which a representative of one of the major faiths is invited to deliver a short, reflective piece with a moral lesson in it for listeners to consider. They are generally pretty serious interludes in an otherwise light-hearted show, but I found myself really struggling not to dissolve into nervous hysterics as I introduced him and exchanged pleasantries over the airwaves. I couldn't work out what on earth he was doing, wearing make-up. It's moments like these that can ruin a DJ's reputation for professionalism! It's not every day I find myself broadcasting to millions, talking to a vicar made up as Widow Twanky, but it was the shock and surrealism of it that set me off. He's called the Reverend Roger Royle, and I've since got to know him quite well. He's the world's loveliest, funniest vicar, and does lots of work for the BBC, including many of the funerals. Before delivering his piece, he explained about the make-up: he was appearing in panto somewhere up north, he told me, and hadn't had time to clean up; he had driven through the night like that to get to Broadcasting House.

LYNN PARSONS, disc jockey

Will the Real Father Christmas Please Stand Up?

The Origins of Santa Claus

ST NICHOLAS IS PROBABLY THE MOST popular of the 10,000 or so saints venerated by Christians, and yet we know virtually nothing about him. There are more chapels and churches named after him than any of the 12 Apostles, including 500 in England alone. Today, his name conjures up an image of a jolly *bon viveur* with a weakness for brandy and cakes, but the real St Nicholas was nothing like his modern-day manifestation: he was a **pious, serious-minded, abstemious** monk, who shunned wealth and materialism and spent much of his life travelling the Middle East and helping the poor. There are all sorts of legends and tales about St Nicholas, most of which are nonsense, but they have been repeated so often over the centuries, and in so many different recesses of the Christian Church, that some probably contain small elements of the truth. What we know for certain is that he was born at Parara, a city in Asia Minor (modern-day Turkey); he grew up in a wealthy family but gave away all the money he inherited; he made a pilgrimage to Egypt and Palestine as a young man; he was appointed Bishop of Myra, also in Asia Minor; he was imprisoned during the persecution of Christians under the Roman emperor Diocletian, and he was released after the accession of Constantine, famously the first emperor to convert to Christianity. He died on 6 December (his feast day) in AD 345 or 352. In 1087 Italian sailors stole his body from Myra and brought it back to the Italian port of Bari where he is now kept in the cathedral named after him. On his feast day, local sailors still carry his statue from the cathedral out to sea, in the hope that his blessing will protect them in the coming year.

Behold the maiestie and grace
of loueing. cheerfull, Christmas face.
Whome many thousands with one breath:
Cry, out let him be put to death.
Who indeede can neuer die:
So long as man hath memory.

❄ ❄ ❄ ❄

BY THE START OF THE RENAISSANCE, NICHOLAS WAS WELL ESTABLISHED as the **most popular saint** in Europe. Even after the Reformation, when Protestants sought to suppress the veneration of saints and other icons, his popularity remained undimmed, especially in the Netherlands. It was there that 'Sinter Klaas' began his slow transformation from austere Asian monk into the jovial figure from the North Pole we recognize today. Early depictions of St Nicholas show him wearing long flowing robes, sometimes in red, which perhaps explains how 'Santa' came to acquire his characteristic red suit.

❄ ❄ ❄ ❄

You know you're getting old when Santa starts looking younger.

ANON

ST NICHOLAS IS THE PATRON SAINT OF DOZENS OF GROUPS OF PEOPLE, as well as several countries, cities and towns. Those claiming the benefit of the great man's patronage include scholars, sailors, merchants, Russians, bakers, Greeks, pawnbrokers, archers, Neapolitans, bankers, jurists, Sicilians, brewers, coopers, travellers, perfumers, unmarried girls, brides and robbers. But it is with young children, of whom he is also the patron saint, that he has been most closely connected over the centuries, although there is no hard evidence of a reason for this association, only ludicrous legends. Perhaps the best known is the story of the three impecunious daughters (see p. 109) whom he rescues from a life of penury by hurling money down their chimneys and straight into their socks as he speeds by their house on his white steed. Another story to leave you stammering in incredulity is the one about him bringing back to life three young boys murdered by an innkeeper, who kept them, for reasons unclear, in a barrel of brine. But there are so many of these tales that it's safe to assume there's a sound historical basis to his reputation as someone who was jolly nice to children.

❄ ❄ ❄ ❄

There's nothing sadder in this world than to awake on Christmas morning and not be a child.
ERMA BOMBECK (1927–96), American humorist

THE NOTION OF ST NICHOLAS AS THE STEALTHY MIDNIGHT DELIVERER of gifts appears to have begun in the Netherlands in the late Middle Ages, but it was on the morning of 6 December, his feast day, that he stole into homes to reward deserving children with presents, and undeserving ones with lumps of coal. When Christmas underwent its dramatic revival in the nineteenth century, the St Nicholas delivery date, in the United States and Britain at least, switched to **Christmas Eve**. No one officially declared that Christmas Eve was stocking-filling night — it just evolved that way, probably because Victorian common sense and practical considerations dictated that it was neater to condense the St Nicholas Day/Advent/Christmas/New Year holidays into a shorter period of time. Hard-working American settlers, grafting Victorian industrialists and empire-builders could hardly be expected to give over the better part of a month to recreation and relaxation.

✳ ✳ ✳ ✳

THE PROTESTANT REFORMATION produced a rival to St Nicholas in the form of the **Christkind** ('Christ Child') or Kris Kringle, as he became known in the States. The Christkind is thought to be a German creation (some claim the idea came from Martin Luther himself) to discourage the Catholic habit of venerating saints like Nicholas. The Christkind is an angel-like figure, who, like St Nicholas, delivers presents to worthy children. In Scandinavia, meanwhile, for centuries parents have been telling children that jolly elves, trolls and gnomes deliver the gifts in a sleigh, drawn by goats or reindeer.

✳ ✳ ✳ ✳

FATHER CHRISTMAS IS NOT just the British name for Santa Claus; he is a fictional character who emerges from the late medieval period, whose true origins may even pre-date Christianity.

The American Santa Claus has one principal source of origin: the Dutch settlers who brought their veneration of Sinter Klaas with them to the New World. But in Britain, the modern-day character of Father Christmas is an amalgamation of Sinter Klaas and a more mysterious, uncertain figure from Norse and other pagan mythology, dating back to heaven only knows when, and bound up with the winter solstice and the coming of spring. Typically, he wore a long, hooded cloak and was festooned with evergreen wreaths of holly, ivy or mistletoe. In Britain, we would recognize him as a version of the **Green Man**. But the existence of this pagan character is disputed by some historians, who point out that there is not a shred of hard evidence to support him. Some even claim paganists invented him in the last 200 years or so to add weight to the canon of their beliefs.

Supporters of the pagan Father Christmas theory say that his story, like other pagan characters and customs, has been passed down the years through the oral tradition from a time when the only writings were those produced by a handful of monks concentrating exclusively on the Christian experience.

❊ ❊ ❊ ❊

THE REINDEER IS VITALLY important to the **nomadic tribes** of the Arctic regions, especially the Lapps. The only deer that can be domesticated provides fat, meat, cheese, clothing, footwear, tools and transport. The antlers and bones are used to make the tools and the sinews are used to make highly durable bindings.

❊ ❊ ❊ ❊

CENTURIES OF HUNTING AND THE gradual **destruction of its natural habitat** by man — much of it through the construction of hydroelectric power plants

— have combined to cause major problems for reindeer in the Arctic. The lands on which they have roamed for millennia have shrunk in size, the migration routes have been disrupted and their population has dropped sharply.

❄ ❄ ❄ ❄

IN DAYS GONE BY, FINNS USED to measure distance by the length a reindeer can run without having a pee. The measurement is known as *poronkusema*, which, no surprises, means 'reindeer pissing' and is thought to cover a distance of between seven and ten kilometres. Reindeer cannot pee while they're moving.

❄ ❄ ❄ ❄

THERE IS NO LAND BENEATH THE Arctic ice cap covering the North Pole, unlike its equivalent in the southern hemisphere. The sea ice is between two and three metres thick, and its total area halves in size during the summer months. In 2004, an international team of 300 scientists published an alarming report into the impact of global warming on the Arctic ice pack, which, they claim, will reduce by as much as 50 per cent by the end of the century. The **big meltdown** will cause sea levels to rise so high they will flood many low-lying lands around the world, and they may even alter the currents of the oceans and regional climates, raising fears that Britain may be plunged into a mini Ice Age.

❄ ❄ ❄ ❄

THERE ARE EIGHTY PEOPLE listed in the telephone directory across the United States under the name S. Claus.

❄ ❄ ❄ ❄

A DAY-OLD REINDEER CALF CAN outsprint a man.

❄ ❄ ❄ ❄

REINDEER ARE THE ONLY SPECIES of deer in which the **females have horns** — an evolutionary quirk that helps them compete with males for the meagre food supplies in their harsh environment.

THE FIRST WRITTEN REFERENCES TO THE pagan Father Christmas figure begin to surface in the 1400s, where he appears frequently in the traditional mummers' plays performed in England over the Christmas period. A fifteenth-century carol includes the line 'Welcome, my lord Christmas'. In Tudor and Stuart times he is referred to as Sir Christmas, Captain Christmas or Old Christmas. Whatever his name or guise, Christmas was always **cheerful, generous, amusing, overweight and bearded**. The first image of Father Christmas comes in 1638 in the form of an illustration by writer Thomas Nabbes, who depicted him as an old man in a furred coat and cap. When the Puritans banned Christmas celebrations in the mid-seventeenth century, Father Christmas 'went dark', as the spies say, and emerged as a powerful allegorical figure, representing the outlawed festivities and mocking the new authorities.

❋ ❋ ❋ ❋

IT WAS DURING THE EARLY NINETEENTH CENTURY THAT ST NICHOLAS and Father Christmas began to merge into the Santa Claus character we recognize today. **Dutch settlers** on the eastern seaboard of the United States, most notably in New York, made something of a public show of celebrating St Nicholas's feast day on 6 December, and there are a number of engravings from that time showing the saint in a hat and robes, with images of stockings full of gifts and fruit hung at the fireside. It was, however, still very much an exclusively Dutch tradition to which no one else, bar a handful of satirists and mickey-takers, paid much attention.

❋ ❋ ❋ ❋

SANTA CLAUS WASN'T BORN, HE EVOLVED, BUT IF WE HAD TO GIVE HIM a birthday it would be 23 December 1822. The man responsible for introducing the Santa we recognize today into the heart of the Western Christmas experience was a strait-laced Episcopalian minister and classical scholar called **Clement Clark Moore**. Little could Moore have known at the time that his fame would be based, not on any of his lifetime labours, but on a piece of borderline doggerel, which he dashed off, half asleep, before retiring to bed one night. Until then, Moore was best known for a hefty two-volume work entitled *A Compendious Lexicon of the Hebrew Language*. The

New York professor supposedly wrote his famous poem, 'An Account of a Visit from St Nicholas', on the evening of the 23rd and read it to his three daughters the following night, just a few hours before St Nick and the eight reindeer he depicted parked up on the family roof. Thus, with a blast of imaginative thinking and a few strokes of his pen, the professor transformed an ascetic Turkish monk into a **fat, slightly camp old man** with a dubious dress sense and a whiff of brandy on his beard, blessed with the extraordinary ability to traverse the globe in a single day, flying from house to house in a sleigh drawn by reindeer, descending chimneys and dispensing gifts to good children throughout the Christian world. It was fortunate perhaps that the serious-minded and austere St Nicholas was no longer alive to witness his extraordinary transformation. A woman friend of the Moore family liked the poem so much that she sent a copy to the *Troy Sentinel* newspaper, who published it the following year. The fact that it was published anonymously has provided the basis for some not very convincing conspiracy theories that Moore was not the poem's author. (It was John F. Kennedy, apparently.) In truth, Moore was a respected scholar with a reputation to uphold, who was probably trying to distance himself from such a frivolous piece of work.

❄ ❄ ❄ ❄

IN THE 1860S, THOMAS NAST, THE FATHER OF AMERICAN POLITICAL cartooning, produced a string of famous illustrations inspired by Moore's poem that succeeded in entrenching Santa's image in the mind of the public. Published in the popular *Harper's Weekly*, the illustrations depict a **short, almost troll-like figure**, with a full white beard, portly frame and fur-trimmed suit, clutching a pile of toys under his arm with a sack on his back and a pipe in his mouth. But for a handful of modifications, the image of Santa Claus has changed remarkably little in almost 150 years. His long pipe has been lost over the years to the forces of political correctness and he's grown a few inches over the decades, but otherwise Nast's likeness is one that we would recognize today. A famous Coca-Cola advert of 1931 once and for all established red as the standard colour for Father Christmas's suit. The illustrator Haddon Sundblum also added a black belt and black boots.

'Twas the night before Christmas, when all through the house
Not a creature was stirring, not even a mouse.
The stockings were hung by the chimney with care,
In hopes that St Nicholas soon would be there.
The children were nestled all snug in their beds,
While visions of sugar-plums danced through their heads,
And mamma in her kerchief, and I in my cap,
Had just settled our brains for a long winter's nap,
When out on the lawn there arose such a clatter,
I sprang from the bed to see what was the matter.
Away to the window I flew like a flash,
Tore open the shutters and threw up the sash.
The moon, on the breast of the new-fallen snow
Gave a lustre of mid-day to objects below;
When, what to my wondering eyes should appear,
But a miniature sleigh, and eight tiny reindeer.
With a little old driver, so lively and quick,
I knew in a moment it must be St Nick.
More rapid than eagles his coursers they came,
And he whistled, and shouted, and called them by name!
'Now Dasher! now, Dancer! now, Prancer and Vixen!
On, Comet! On, Cupid! on, on Donner and Blitzen!
To the top of the porch! to the top of the wall!
Now dash away! Dash away! Dash away all!'
As dry leaves that before the wild hurricane fly,
When they meet with an obstacle, mount to the sky,
So up to the house-top the coursers they flew,
With a sleigh full of toys, and St Nicholas too.

And then, in a twinkling, I heard on the roof
The prancing and pawing of each little hoof.
As I drew in my head, and was turning around,
Down the chimney St Nicholas came with a bound.
He was dressed all in fur, from his head to his foot,
And his clothes were all tarnished with ashes and soot.
A bundle of toys he had flung on his back,
And he looked like a peddler, just opening his pack.
His eyes — how they twinkled! his dimples how merry!
His cheeks were like roses, his nose like a cherry!
His droll little mouth was drawn up like a bow,
And the beard of his chin was as white as the snow.
The stump of a pipe he held tight in his teeth,
And the smoke it encircled his head like a wreath.
He had a broad face and a little round belly,
That shook when he laughed, like a bowlful of jelly.
He was chubby and plump, a right jolly old elf,
And I laughed when I saw him, in spite of myself!
A wink of his eye and a twist of his head,
Soon gave me to know I had nothing to dread.
He spoke not a word, but went straight to his work,
And filled all the stockings; then turned with a jerk,
And laying his finger aside of his nose,
And giving a nod, up the chimney he rose!
He sprang to his sleigh, to his team gave a whistle,
And away they all flew like the down of a thistle.
But I heard him exclaim, 'ere he drove out of sight,
'Happy Christmas to all, and to all a good-night!'

CLEMENT CLARK MOORE (1779–1863), 'An Account of a Visit from St Nicholas'

MOORE'S POEM HAS spawned scores of parodies, many of them very clever, some obscene, but most just plain silly. Writing them and circulating them on the web, or by email, has become something of an American Christmas custom in its own right. Below and on p. 160 are two of the more amusing ones:

The Night Before Christmas, Legally Speaking

Whereas, on or about the night prior to Christmas, there did occur at a certain improved piece of real property (hereinafter 'the House') a general lack of stirring by all creatures therein, including, but not limited to, a mouse.

A variety of foot apparel, e.g. stocking, socks, etc., had been affixed by and around the chimney in said House in the hope and/or belief that St Nick aka St Nicholas aka Santa Claus (hereinafter 'Claus') would arrive at sometime thereafter.

The minor residents, i.e. the children, of the aforementioned House were located in their individual beds and were engaged in nocturnal hallucinations, i.e. dreams, wherein vision of confectionery treats, including, but not limited to, candies, nuts and/or sugar plums, did dance, cavort and otherwise appear in said dreams.

Whereupon the party of the first part (sometimes hereinafter referred to as 'I'), being the joint-owner in fee simple of the House with the parts of the second part (hereinafter 'Mamma'), and said Mamma had retired for a sustained period of sleep. (At such time, the parties were clad in various forms of headgear, e.g. kerchief and cap.)

Suddenly, and without prior notice or warning, there did occur upon the unimproved real property adjacent and appurtenant to said House, i.e. the lawn, a certain disruption of unknown nature, cause and/or circumstance. The party of the first part did immediately rush to a window in the House to investigate the cause of such disturbance.

At that time, the party of the first part did observe, with some degree of wonder and/or disbelief, a miniature sleigh (hereinafter 'the Vehicle') being pulled and/or drawn very rapidly through the air by approximately eight (8) reindeer. The driver of the

Vehicle appeared to be and in fact was, the previously referenced Claus.

Said Claus was providing specific direction, instruction and guidance to the approximately eight (8) reindeer and specifically identified the animal co-conspirators by name: Dasher, Dancer, Prancer, Vixen, Comet, Cupid, Donner and Blitzen (hereinafter 'the Deer'). (Upon information and belief, it is further asserted that an additional co-conspirator named 'Rudolph' may have been involved.)

The party of the first part witnessed Claus, the Vehicle and the Deer intentionally and willfully trespass upon the roofs of several residences located adjacent to and in the vicinity of the House, and noted that the Vehicle was heavily laden with packages, toys and other items of unknown origin or nature. Suddenly, without prior invitation or permission, either express or implied, the Vehicle arrived at the House, and Claus entered said House via the chimney.

Said Claus was clad in a red fur suit, which was partially covered with residue from the chimney, and he carried a large sack containing a portion of the aforementioned packages, toys, and other unknown items. He was smoking what appeared to be tobacco in a small pipe in blatant violation of local ordinances and health regulations.

Claus did not speak, but immediately began to fill the stocking of the minor children, which hung adjacent to the chimney, with toys and other small gifts. (Said items did not, however, constitute 'gifts' to said minors pursuant to the applicable provisions of the U.S. Tax Code.)

Upon completion of such task, Claus touched the side of his nose and flew, rose and/or ascended up the chimney of the House to the roof where the Vehicle and Deer waited and/or served as 'lookouts.' Claus immediately departed for an unknown destination.

However, prior to the departure of the Vehicle, Deer and Claus from said House, the party of the first part did hear Claus state and/or exclaim: 'Merry Christmas to all and to all a good night!' Or words to that effect.

AUTHOR UNKNOWN

✳ ✳ ✳ ✳

The one thing women don't want to find in their stockings on Christmas morning is their husband.

JOAN RIVERS (1933–),
American comedian

The Cat Before Christmas

Twas the night before Christmas and all through the house
Not a creature was stirring, not even a mouse.
Cos the cat had pounced on him and tore him apart
Ate his mousey intestines and chewed up his heart.
Kitty thought he heard sleigh bells, which made him take pause
He stopped daintily licking the blood from his claws.
'Must be Santa,' thought Kitty, that quite clever cat
'Cos nobody else climbs down the chimney like that.'
Indeed it was ol' Santa, so jolly and fat
With a load of presents, and all for the cat!
'Wow, the best Christmas ever!' Kitty thought with a purr,
Then he coughed up a hairball and shed some more fur.

AUTHOR UNKNOWN

❄ ❄ ❄ ❄

RUDOLPH, THE MOST FAMOUS REINDEER OF ALL, ENTERED THE world more than a century after Clement Clark Moore gave us Dasher, Dancer, Prancer and Vixen. The shy one with the **bright red nose**, who showed the world that a facial abnormality is no bar to career advancement or a happy life, was the brainchild of American copywriter Robert L. May. He came up with the Rudolph narrative poem in 1939 as a way of attracting more customers into the Montgomery Ward chain of department stores. The poem sold more than two million copies that year and when it was republished in 1946, after the Second World War, the book sold another three and a half million.

❄ ❄ ❄ ❄

DEPARTMENT STORE SANTA CLAUSES WITH real white bushy beards earn up to twice as much as their colleagues with imitation beards.

NEVER TRUST A MAN WITH A BEARD, THEY SAY ... ER, EXCEPT SANTA Claus. **Fear of facial hair** (other people's) is a surprisingly common phobia affecting the health and lifestyle of thousands of people around the world, according to experts. Pogonophobia is defined as 'a persistent, abnormal, and unwarranted fear of beards' that apparently can cause profound distress to sufferers. (You can only imagine the suffering of pogonophobes in Victorian times – the Golden Age of the Beard – especially if they were soldiers serving in beard-crazy Afghanistan or the Punjab. There can't have been a clean-shaven face for hundreds of miles!) The CTRN Phobia Clinic is an American organization that claims to have helped presidents, royals, celebrities and top sportsmen overcome their phobias. (CTRN stands for 'Change That's Right Now'.) Reading the company's literature, it becomes clear that pogonophobia is not something we should be sniggering into our beards about at all, in fact. Read this and you will never laugh about facial hair again:

... the problem often significantly impacts the quality of life. It can cause panic attacks and keep people apart from loved ones and business associates. Symptoms typically include shortness of breath, rapid breathing, irregular heartbeat, sweating, nausea, and overall feelings of dread, although everyone experiences pogonophobia in their own way and may have different symptoms. Though a variety of potent drugs are often prescribed for pogonophobia, side effects and/or withdrawal symptoms can be severe. Moreover, drugs do not 'cure' pogonophobia or any other phobia. At best they temporarily suppress the symptoms through chemical interaction ...

If you are living with pogonophobia, what is the real cost to your health, your career or school, and to your family life? Avoiding the issue indefinitely would mean resigning yourself to living in fear, missing out on priceless life experiences big and small, living a life that is just a shadow of what it will be when the problem is gone.

For anyone earning a living, the financial toll of this phobia is incalculable. Living with fear means you can never concentrate fully and give your best. Lost opportunities. Poor performance or grades. Promotions that pass you by. Pogonophobia will likely cost you tens, even hundreds of thousands of dollars over the course of your lifetime, let alone the cost to your health and quality of life. Like all fears and phobias, pogonophobia is created by the unconscious mind as a protective mechanism. At some point in your past, there was likely an event linking beards and emotional trauma. Whilst the original catalyst may have been a real-life scare of some kind, the condition can also be triggered by myriad benign events like movies, TV, or perhaps seeing someone else experience trauma.

IF SANTA'S SLEIGH WAS LOADED WITH ONE BARBIE DOLL AND ONE Action Man for every girl and boy on the planet it would weigh **400,000 tons** and need almost a billion reindeer to pull it. To deliver all his presents in one global night-time, Santa would have to deliver to roughly 1,500 homes a second and, allowing for chimney descents and mince-pie breaks, he and the reindeer would have to travel at roughly 5,000 times the speed of sound. I understand from my contacts in the aviation industry that aircraft would burst into flames at just a fraction of that speed.

❄ ❄ ❄ ❄

THE FOLLOWING WAS FIRST PRINTED ON THE EDITORIAL PAGE OF THE *New York Sun* newspaper on 21 September 1897 under the headline: **Yes, Virginia, There Is A Santa Claus!**

We take pleasure in answering thus prominently the communication below, expressing at the same time our great gratification that its faithful author is numbered among the friends of The Sun:

'I am 8 years old. Some of my little friends say there is no Santa Claus. Papa says, "If you see it in The Sun, *it's so." Please tell me the truth, is there a Santa Claus?' Virginia O'Hanlon*

Virginia, your little friends are wrong. They have been affected by the scepticism of a sceptical age. They do not believe except for what they see. They think that nothing can be which is not comprehensible by their little minds. All minds, Virginia, whether they be men's or children's, are little. In this great universe of ours, man is a mere insect, an ant, in his intellect as compared with the boundless world about him, as measured by the intelligence capable of grasping the whole of truth and knowledge.

Yes, Virginia, there is a Santa Claus.

He exists as certainly as love and generosity and devotion exist, and you know that they abound and give to your life its highest beauty and joy. Alas! How dreary would be the world if there were no Santa Claus! It would be as dreary as if there were no Virginias. There would be no childlike faith then, no poetry, no romance to make tolerable this existence. We should have no enjoyment, except in sense and sight. The external light with which childhood fills the world would be extinguished.

Not believe in Santa Claus! You might as well not believe in fairies. You might get your papa to hire men to watch in all the chimneys on Christmas eve to catch Santa Claus, but even if you did not see Santa Claus coming down, what would that prove? Nobody sees Santa Claus, but that is no sign that there is no Santa Claus. The most real things in the world are those that neither children nor

men can see. Did you ever see fairies dancing on the lawn? Of course not, but that's no proof that they are not there. Nobody can conceive or imagine all the wonders there are unseen and unseeable in the world.

You tear apart the baby's rattle and see what makes the noise inside, but there is a veil covering the unseen world which not the strongest man, nor even the united strength of all the strongest men that ever lived could tear apart. Only faith, poetry, love, romance, can push aside that curtain and view and picture the supernatural beauty and glory beyond. Is it all real? Ah, Virginia, in all this world there is nothing else real and abiding.

No Santa Claus? Thank God he lives and lives forever. A thousand years from now, Virginia, nay 10 times 10,000 years from now, he will continue to make glad the heart of childhood.

Merry Christmas and a Happy New Year!

THE FIREFIGHTER

WHEN I WAS YOUNG AND HAD NO CHILDREN I USED TO LOVE WORKING the Christmas Day shift. You got double money and there was often some overtime to be had because in those days there were always call-outs at Christmas, generally later in the day when people had had a few drinks and got a bit careless. Today, thanks to our emphasis on education and the installation of more and more smoke alarms, we don't get called out anything like as often. Most of the single firefighters on the brigade, or those without children, used to volunteer to work the day so that the men and women with young families could be at home. In fairness, it was no great sacrifice because there was always a party atmosphere at the station on the day shift.

It seems incredible now but when I joined the Fire Brigade, in the early 1980s, we used to cook up a full turkey lunch with all the trimmings and even the odd bottle of wine or beer. I was looking through some old photo albums recently and was amazed by the pictures I took on Christmas Day 1985, when I was stationed at Ealing in West London. The entire crew were sitting around the table with paper hats on their heads, grinning from ear to ear at the end of what was clearly a highly enjoyable occasion. There were streamers all round the room, two bottles of wine and a few cans of beer on the table and a pile of plates and turkey bones scattered across the surfaces. Such a scene is unimaginable today because our working practices have changed beyond all recognition. For a start, we no longer have the extensive kitchen facilities of old with which to cook a full Christmas feast — at least that's the case in the Staffordshire fire service and I believe it's a similar situation up and down the country. Nowadays people tend to bring in packed lunches, which we generally eat watching the telly rather than congregating around a long table as we once did. There are no longer any beds either, so if you're working the night shift, you have to rest — or try to — on the reclining seats that have recently been provided for us.

Christmas Day is still one of the few Bank Holidays we get, but it's not so much fun these days. In truth, it's just like any other day, a bit depressing even, because you know that your family, and almost everybody else out there, are all at home enjoying themselves. I have three young children of my own now and if I have to work on Christmas Day I prefer to work the day shift, so at least I get to be with them when they tear open their stockings at first light. Watching their joy and excitement is the high point of the day for me. If possible I try not to work overnight on Christmas Eve because that means I don't get back home until mid-morning. If it's been a busy night I'll also be very tired, which isn't great given how busy it gets at home on Christmas Day.

It's a shame that working at Christmas is no longer the boisterous, happy affair it used to be. Apart from the sheer fun of it, you felt a powerful sense of camaraderie with the rest of the crew as we crowded around the table, bantering and making speeches and toasts. From hindsight, I suppose it's remarkable that we were ever allowed to drink on the premises and it was no surprise when they quickly began to phase out alcohol in stations the year after I took that photograph of our Christmas lunch — a ruling hastened by a drink-drive incident involving a firefighter in one of the London crews. Like us at Ealing, his crew had enjoyed a traditional Christmas lunch but when they were called out later in the day the driver of one of the engines must have been a little ragged around the edges and managed to crash, first into a pharmacy and then into a parked car, provoking a furious response from the car's owner. The pharmacy was located at the bottom of a block of flats and all the occupants of the building had to be evacuated amid fears for its structural safety. To make matters worse, the driver ran away and when police later caught up with him at home, he was breathalysed and found to be twice the old legal limit, although he claimed that he only started drinking *after* the crash. It being a quiet day for news, the incident found its way into the headlines of the national newspapers.

The great majority of us, however, were very sensible about drinking on Christmas Day, not least because we spend much of our working lives attending to fires, crashes and incidents that have been caused by alcohol, but some crews had a reputation for enjoying their drink more than others. It was reasonable and inevitable to ban drinking on the job and, in the wider scheme of things, missing out on a traditional Christmas lunch is, I suppose, a small hardship to bear. Today, each of the four crews has a Christmas 'office party' at a restaurant, generally a curry house, just like everyone else, but somehow it's not quite the same.

RANDLE WILBRAHAM

Staffordshire Fire and Rescue Service

Moon Orbits, Tsunamis and Train Crashes:

News Stories That Shook Christmas

AT 7.15 PM ON 28 December 1879, the newly constructed **Tay Bridge** at Dundee collapsed into the river below during a severe storm, taking with it a six-carriage train with approximately 75 passengers on board. There were no survivors. At just over two miles in length, the Tay was the longest bridge in the world at the time, and its construction provoked great excitement in Victorian society. Designed by Thomas Bouch, who was knighted for his efforts, the bridge took six years to build and was opened, amid great fanfare, in May 1878. Six hundred labourers, 20 of whom died in the construction, used over ten million bricks and two million rivets to build it. Investigations into the collapse laid the blame on Bouch's poor design. The tragedy caused an outpouring of grief and shock across the country and was responsible for what many people regard as the worst well-known poem in the English language, written by the world's worst poet, William McGonagall. The simple title 'The Tay Bridge Disaster' gives no indication of the poetic horrors that follow. Doctors recommend that only small passages of the poem be read at a time, so below I have laid out merely the first and last stanzas for your enjoyment. Deep breaths now.

Beautiful railway bridge of the Silv'ry Tay!
Alas! I am very sorry to say
That ninety lives have been taken away
On the last Sabbath day of 1879,
Which will be remember'd for a very long time …

It must have been an awful sight,
To witness in the dusky moonlight,
While the Storm Fiend did laugh, and angry did bray,
Along the Railway Bridge of the Silv'ry Tay,
Oh! ill-fated Bridge of the Silv'ry Tay,
I must now conclude my lay
By telling the world fearlessly without the least dismay,
That your central girders would not have given way,
At least many sensible men do say,
Had they been supported on each side with buttresses,
At least many sensible men confesses,
For the stronger we our houses do build,
The less chance we have of being killed.

❄ ❄ ❄ ❄

ON 26 DECEMBER 1908, AMERICAN BOXER **JACK JOHNSON** STRUCK A blow for racial equality when he became the first black heavyweight world champion by knocking out Canadian Tommy Burns in the 14th round of their fight in Sydney, Australia. Johnson had followed Burns all over the world, demanding a contest and taunting him in the press. The fight was stopped by the police after Johnson had handed out a severe beating to his opponent. Ever controversial, Johnson – the most famous black man on the planet for two decades – goaded Burns and his ringside team throughout the bout. Barely anyone in the 20,000-strong crowd cheered the American as he dominated Burns. Each time Burns looked like he was going to collapse, Johnson held him up so that he could hammer him more. Johnson, who received a tepid welcome on his return to the United States, had defeated a string of challengers to keep his title when, in 1910, he came face to face with Jim Jeffries, the Great White Hope. Jeffries came out of retirement to try to beat the controversial and flamboyant Johnson. During the contest at Reno, Nevada, Johnson became the first boxer to knock down Jeffries, whose corner threw in the towel in the 15th round. Johnson's victory triggered racial violence and rioting across the United States.

ON 28 DECEMBER 1908, ITALY was in the middle of its long Christmas holidays when **the worst earthquake** in European history, followed by a giant tsunami, brought immeasurable devastation to the south of the country. Hundreds of buildings collapsed when the quake struck the Messina Strait which separates Calabria from Sicily, at 5.30 in the morning. Tens of thousands were entombed in their homes as they slept, while many others were killed by falling buildings as they fled into the streets. Estimates of the death toll vary but most agree that the figure was not less than 200,000. The towns of Messina (population 150,000) and Reggio Calabria (50,000), the biggest in the region, were razed to the ground by a quake that would measure roughly 7.5 on the modern Richter scale.

❄ ❄ ❄ ❄

FRANCE'S WORST PEACETIME railway disaster took place two days before Christmas in 1933 when the country's largest locomotive, travelling at over 60mph, rammed into the rear of a stationary train standing at Lagny-Pomponne station, 17 miles from Paris. The **horrendous crash**, which killed 238 people and injured over 300, was blamed on the driver of the Strasbourg express, who ignored several signals in a bid to make up lost time. Such was the impact of the collision that many of the wooden coaches were reduced to splinters. The giant locomotive was later repaired and returned to service, and was dubbed **'Le Charcutier'** (the butcher) by dry-witted railway engineers. The worst rail disaster of the twentieth century had also happened in France, in 1917, when a military train derailed as it headed into a tunnel in the Alps. Officially, 540 people died, but other estimates suggest the figure was closer to 800.

* * * *

NEW ZEALAND WAS PLUNGED into mourning on Christmas Eve 1953 when a flood triggered by minor volcanic activity swept away a train on a bridge. One hundred and fifty of the 285 passengers on board, most of them **en route to see Queen Elizabeth II** during her first state visit to the country, died when six of the nine carriages sank to the bottom of the flooded Whangaehu River. In a bizarre sequence of events, the volcanic Mount Ruapehu on the North Island experienced a small eruption, releasing millions of gallons of water from a lake that surged down the mountainside before crashing into the bridge. Destabilized by the torrent of water, the bridge collapsed when the Wellington to Auckland express train crossed it minutes later. Arthur Cyril Ellis, a local postal clerk, tried to warn the approaching train by running down the line and waving his torch. The driver applied the brakes but the train was too close to the bridge.

ON CHRISTMAS EVE 1968 the three astronauts of the Apollo 8 spacecraft became the first manned space mission to orbit the Moon. Watched live by a global television audience, the Americans fired their rocket engine to send Apollo 8 into the first of 10 elliptical lunar orbits. For 45 minutes of each orbit, Apollo 8 passed out of contact with mission control in Houston when it disappeared to the **dark side of the moon**, which had never previously been seen by man. During the orbits, the astronauts – Frank Borman, James Lovell and William Anders – sent back the television pictures of what they were seeing. They also quoted from the Book of Genesis, describing the creation of the world. The astronauts struggled to sleep during the three-day voyage, complaining that as they could not rest their heads in the weightless atmosphere they kept jerking themselves awake, thinking that they were falling. Early in the flight, Borman fell sick, vomiting twice and suffering a bout of diarrhoea, which filled the spacecraft with globules of sick and faeces. On Christmas Day the astronauts opened their food lockers to discover a meal of real turkey with stuffing and three miniature bottles of brandy, together with some presents from their wives. After splashing down in the Pacific on 27 December, they were picked up by the aircraft carrier *Yorktown* and returned to the United States as national heroes.

❄ ❄ ❄ ❄

DEATH, DESTRUCTION, CIVIL UNREST AND DISEASE VISITED THE Nicaraguan capital of Managua during the Christmas holiday period of 1972 after a 6.2-magnitude earthquake killed 10,000 people and left a quarter of a million homeless. Three-quarters of the city was destroyed when the earthquake struck in the dead of night, wiping out all electricity, gas, water, sewage and telephone systems in a matter of seconds. **The tremors continued for hours** as hundreds of fires broke out across the capital, which was built on poor soil over four significant fault lines. With thousands of dead and dying left under the rubble, President Somoza Debyale ordered an immediate evacuation of the city and the imposition of martial law as chaos erupted. Four major hospitals were destroyed in the quake, leaving thousands of casualties without medical treatment. Bodies were burned in the streets to prevent the spread of disease. In the clean-up operation, most of the city was bulldozed with the bodies of the dead still in the rubble.

❄ ❄ ❄ ❄

CHRISTMAS JOY TURNED TO DESPAIR FOR THE CITIZENS OF DARWIN when **Cyclone Tracy** reduced the Australian city to rubble on 25 December 1974. Incredibly, only 65 people were killed in one of the country's worst natural disasters, even though 9,000 homes and 90 per cent of the city were destroyed in the raging storm. Thousands of people were left homeless after winds touching 140mph and torrential rain crashed into the country's northern coast. In the week following Christmas Day, over 25,000 people were flown out of the city and a further 10,000 escaped by road, leaving a population of just 10,000 amid the ruins and floodwater.

THE CORNISH FISHING COMMUNITY OF **MOUSEHOLE** SPENT CHRISTMAS 1981 in mourning after eight local lifeboatmen were drowned answering an emergency call in a violent storm. The crew of the *Solomon Browne* launched in a Force-12 hurricane with winds gusting at almost 100 knots and waves towering as high as sixty feet. Many of the crew had been socializing in the British Legion club when the distress signal was received, and conditions were so bad that it was decided only one volunteer from each family should go. The RNLI boat was attempting to assist the stricken *Union Star*, which was being driven towards the rocky coastline to a certain destruction. There were eight people aboard the coaster – on her maiden voyage from Denmark to Ireland – including the captain's pregnant wife and his two stepdaughters. Reports suggested that the lifeboatmen, at huge risk to their own lives, had managed to rescue four people when disaster struck. The following morning, searchers found the lifeboat smashed into small pieces against the cliffs, while the *Union Star* had been flipped upside down and was stuck on the rocks. Posthumous awards were made to the lifeboat crew for what was regarded as exceptional gallantry, even by the high standards of the RNLI.

ON 17 DECEMBER 1983, ONE OF THE BUSIEST SHOPPING DAYS OF THE year, an IRA car bomb exploded outside **Harrods** department store in central London killing six people, including three policemen, and injuring 90. The area was packed with Christmas shoppers as the blast tore through the streets and filled the air with a cloud of black smoke.

BRITAIN SUFFERED ITS WORST TERRORIST OUTRAGE AND AVIATION disaster on 21 December 1988 when **Pan Am flight 103** was blown up over the Scottish border, killing all 259 people on board and 11 on the ground. The jumbo jet, en route to New York from London Heathrow, burst into flames at about 31,000ft following the explosion of a bomb, planted in a suitcase by a Libyan secret agent. The wreckage from the plane was littered over 800 square miles, though much of it rained down on the Scottish village of Lockerbie. The impact of the plane hitting the ground registered 1.6 on the Richter scale. The police investigation was the biggest ever mounted in Scotland.

❄ ❄ ❄ ❄

GERMANY HAD PLENTY TO CHEER ABOUT OVER CHRISTMAS 1989 AFTER the Brandenburg Gate was opened for the first time in almost three decades on 22 December, officially ending the bitter division between the east and west of the country. Tens of thousands of elated Germans took to the streets in driving rain to witness the ceremony at one of the most powerful symbols of Cold War division. West German Chancellor Helmut Kohl walked through a tunnel in the Gate to be greeted by Hans Modrow, the prime minister of East Germany. Minutes later the gates were opened and thousands of people poured across the old border, waving, kissing and hugging each other, while others clambered on to the top of the Berlin Wall chanting 'Deutschland!' Addressing the enormous crowd, Kohl declared the historic occasion the 'most important moment of my life'.

❄ ❄ ❄ ❄

BY FAR THE WORST NATURAL DISASTER IN RECENT TIMES TOOK PLACE on Boxing Day 2004 when a **tsunami**, triggered by a powerful earthquake under the Indian Ocean, killed almost a quarter of a million in southern Asia. The 8.9-magnitude earthquake forced up a long section of the ocean floor by about 10 metres, creating an enormous sea surge that sent waves racing towards land at speeds touching 500mph. The north Indonesian coast, close to the quake's epicentre, bore the brunt of the world's largest tsunami for 40 years when it crashed ashore, without any warning, in mid-morning. The giant body of water spread rapidly in all directions, devastating the resort coasts of Sri Lanka and Thailand and the fishing communities of southern India. The tsunami also caused deaths further afield in Malaysia, the Maldives and the Seychelles and was even felt thousands of miles away on the east coast of Africa. Tens of thousands of people watched their loved ones being swept out to sea, and the bodies of many of the dead have never been found. The exact death toll will never be known but more than 200,000 people in 13 countries – roughly 130,000 in Indonesia – have been certified as dead or missing. The tragedy shocked the world, triggering a flood of grief and charity that led to the donation of over eight billion pounds to help with relief and reconstruction efforts.

THE LIFEBOATMAN

I WASN'T MANNING THE STATION ON CHRISTMAS DAY BUT AS ALWAYS I WAS
on call. Although there's plenty of commercial shipping going up and
down the Channel, you don't expect many others to be out at sea. But
just as I was settling down for a quiet end to the day the coastguard at
Dover paged me; he had received a 999 call from someone on top of
the cliffs at Beachy Head. The caller had been out walking his dog in
the fading light when he heard voices shouting for help. He looked
down from the cliff's edge and saw two people stuck on a ledge about
halfway up the cliffs, which are about 500 feet high. It was clear that
they had been cut off by the tides and had thought they could climb to
safety. Right at the bottom the cliffs are not so steep. They suddenly
become sheer, however, as this couple had discovered. They were lucky:
it was almost dark when they were finally heard, and it was unlikely that
anyone else would have come along later. Two local coastguard teams
had gone up to the cliff tops in their Land Rovers, and decided it would
be safest to winch a man down to the ledge. From there he could take
them one by one down to an RNLI boat. The weather wasn't too bad,
but the dark was sure to pose some problems.

The centre of Eastbourne was very quiet when I drove off and
it took me only about five minutes to travel the three miles to the
station for the all-weather lifeboat. The inshore lifeboat is located
nearer the town centre and the crews for both had been paged
at the same time as I had. There was a pretty impressive turnout
considering it was Christmas Day. All eight crew for the all-weather
boat, all six for the inshore boat and 14 shore helpers were ready to
get going within minutes of the alarm being raised. We all knew what
to do. The training just kicks in. My job as coxswain is to drive the
bigger, all-weather boat and take command of the operation at sea.

It took us about 20 minutes to get to Beachy Head, but the faster
inshore boat had arrived 10 minutes ahead and had located the stranded
couple with their searchlights. It was made easier for them because luckily
the couple had brought a torch with them. There wasn't much we could
do at first except stand clear and keep our powerful lights on them while
the coastguard teams on the cliffs rigged up their winches. It's a fairly
straightforward routine which involves digging spikes deep into the earth
and then attaching rolling winches to them before lowering the man over.

What quickly became apparent was that the woman had slipped
and tumbled about 60 feet down the nearly sheer slope before

getting wedged in a gully. This was very, very lucky for her because if she had kept falling she wouldn't have survived. This realization increased the pressure on us because we didn't know if she had been injured. Either way, she would have been very badly shaken up. The good news was that we could see that both were wearing warm clothing. For some reason, I had been expecting the couple to be very young. I was a little surprised to discover they were in their fifties.

We kept one of our lights trained on the coastguard as he was winched down to the woman, attached his harness to her and then continued down to the foot of the cliffs. The smaller inshore lifeboat was waiting at the water's edge to collect her and bring her over to us, before returning to pick up her partner. As they were lifted aboard you could tell both of them had been very frightened, but there was a huge sense of relief too. The woman confessed that the worst part of the whole experience was the seasickness she had begun to feel while waiting on the boat! 'Well, there's just no pleasing some people is there?' joked one of the lads in the crew. 'You pluck someone off a cliff ledge and the next thing they're moaning about the motion of the rescue boat!'

'Merry Christmas!' one of the crew members said as he pulled the man aboard. 'Bah humbug, more like!' he replied. We wrapped them both up in thick blankets and gave them a cup of hot tea as we began to make our way home. By five o'clock we were back at the station, which was pretty impressive considering that just 90 minutes earlier we had all been snoozing in our armchairs or tucking into our turkey roast. It was a good team effort. A paramedic checked the couple over before we dropped them back at their car, and they were able to drive home to London. We don't see it as our role to lecture people about their behaviour, and so we just wished the couple well and went on our way. The coastguard, though, gently commented that they might have been better off waiting a short while for the tide to turn rather than climbing a 500-foot cliff in the gathering darkness. By half past six I was back home, just in time to settle down with the kids and watch *Ghostbusters*.

MARK SAWYER, RNLI

175

Turkey Kebabs and Steamed Goldfish:

Christmas Customs around the World

THE CELEBRATION OF CHRISTMAS, such a joyful event in medieval times, was virtually killed off by the English Puritans, together with their emigrant cousins in North America, and it took the better apart of two centuries for it to recover. Until Victoria married Prince Albert and Dickens picked up his quill, 25 December remained a day of quiet religious observation; the once-boisterous celebrations of the 12-day holiday season were no more than tales of a distant past. For the majority of other Christian cultures around the world, however, this was how it ever was – and continued to be, even following the sensational and sudden revival of Christmas in Britain and the United States in the mid-nineteenth century. The two countries were the most powerful and influential in the world in the second half of that century, and their cultures inevitably filtered into others around the globe, through a combination of colonization, trade networks, the endeavours of Christian missionaries and, latterly, the media. Thus, the Christmas customs of the northern Europeans were exported to the furthest outposts of the planet, bringing curious images of snow-covered reindeer, frosted windows, pine trees and red-faced Santas to the tropics, the deserts, the atolls and the savannahs. Driven by rampant commercialism, this Anglo-German-American version of Christmas has grown in scale and influence around the world, steamrollering and bulldozing many idiosyncratic local and regional customs to destruction, or pushing them to the fringes of their indigenous cultures. The celebration of Christmas has become globalized. Peculiarities and differences remain, but they are not as widespread or pronounced as they once were.

❄ ❄ ❄ ❄

CHRISTMAS DAY IN **ANTARCTICA** is celebrated in 24-hour daylight. In spite of its falling in midsummer, those living there (scientists in snowsuits mainly) can still guarantee a white Christmas — for the time being at least.

THE FIRST OFFICIAL Christmas celebrated in Australia came in 1788 at Sydney Cove, as the British set about establishing the first penal colony on the land claimed for the Crown by Captain Cook a few years earlier. There was, however, little to cheer anyone that year — except convict Michael Dennison. He had been sentenced to **200 lashes** for stealing a pound of flour but, in the festive spirit of peace and goodwill, he had his penalty reduced to just 150 lashes.

❄ ❄ ❄ ❄

A BOILED PIG'S HEAD, OR SNOUT, with mashed-up barley was a Christmas Eve speciality in Latvia for centuries. The dish, known as *kuki*, is not so popular these days.

IN AUSTRALIA, AS IN OTHER SOUTHERN HEMISPHERE COUNTRIES, THE Christmas holiday falls at the height of summer and it's not unusual for people to be carving up the turkey and opening their presents in temperatures touching three figures Fahrenheit. Many Christmas dinners and parties take the form of a **barbecue on the beach** or in the back garden, with the turkey cooked over the coals either whole or in marinated pieces or kebabs. In the absence of snow, many Australian children compromise by making 'sandmen' on the beach.

❄ ❄ ❄ ❄

OVER 70 MAJOR **BUSH FIRES** RAGED ACROSS AUSTRALIA ON CHRISTMAS Day 2001, with 5,000 firefighters on duty and 20,000 helpers preoccupied with containing and extinguishing the blazes. It took over three weeks for the fires to be brought under control.

❄ ❄ ❄ ❄

THE CELEBRATION OF CHRISTMAS IN THE LARGELY CATHOLIC COUNTRIES of South and Central America is a more overtly religious, and less commercial, affair than it has become in Britain and other Western countries. Nativity scenes, street processions and the attendance of church services (especially Midnight Mass) form the focus of the holiday period. In **Brazil** Christmas takes place in the summer and the main feast is eaten outdoors, often on the beach. Many Brazilian cooks marinate their turkey in rum, onions, garlic, tomatoes, lime juice and other spices, and serve it with coloured rice.

❄ ❄ ❄ ❄

IN RECENT TIMES THE CELEBRATION OF CHRISTMAS BY **CHINA'S roughly 50 million Christians** has become a more visible cultural event. Markets and shops have started stocking Western-style Christmas paraphernalia such as cards, trees and traditional gifts as the commercialism of the festival seeps into China's wider community. Children hang up stockings for Dun Che Lao Ren or Lan Khoong (Father Christmas), who can also be found in various shopping malls across the country. Christianity is China's fastest-growing religion but it remains tightly controlled and closely watched by the authorities.

＊ ＊ ＊ ＊

CHRISTMAS WAS **OFFICIALLY ABOLISHED** IN CUBA BY THE COMMUNIST government in 1969, allegedly to avoid any disruption to the all-important sugar harvest. President Castro reinstated the holiday in 1997, but the celebrations have been rather muted as no one under the age of 40 or so has the faintest idea what to do with themselves. Since then, Cuba has experienced a minor religious revival, galvanized by the visit of Pope John Paul II, but Christmas Day still barely registers as an event of significance. Travel the streets of Havana on 25 December, and Christmas decorations remain conspicuous by their absence.

WHILE MANY IN WESTERN EUROPE AND THE UNITED STATES PLUCK and hang their turkeys in preparation for the Christmas feast, the people of the Czech Republic, and others in Eastern Europe, get busy draining their ponds of carp. These **giant goldfish** traditionally form the centrepiece of the Czech Christmas meal and they are often kept in the bathtub until the last minute as they are tastiest when fresh, accompanied by a potato salad. Elsewhere in Central and Eastern Europe, especially in rural areas, the tradition of eating a 12-course meatless meal (one for each apostle) is still observed.

＊ ＊ ＊ ＊

IN **ETHIOPIA**, CHRISTIANS USE THE OLD JULIAN CALENDAR AND celebrate Christmas on 7 January, flocking to the town of Lalibela, built by a king of that name in the twelfth century as Ethiopia's own Jerusalem. Pilgrims travel for days, even weeks, to celebrate the feast day they know as Ganna, which takes its name from a form of hockey believed to have been played by the shepherds as they awaited news of Jesus's birth. Ganna is still played today and forms a big part of the colourful Christmas festivities, which also involve a great deal of singing, dancing and drumming as well as more solemn ceremonies that are conducted in ancient churches carved into hillsides of volcanic rock.

FOR MANY CENTURIES THE SAUNA, A HUGELY IMPORTANT FEATURE of **Finnish culture**, has played a central part in the country's traditional celebration of Christmas. Today Finns still observe the custom of taking a sauna on Christmas Eve, after which many choose to visit the graves of their loved ones before settling down to a lavish dinner. The sauna is an almost sacred institution in Finland and historians now believe that their ancestors were using them as long as 2,000 years ago. There are over **two million saunas** installed throughout the country, the majority of them in private homes. With a population of just five million, the Finns can boast that, by a considerable distance, they have the highest sauna per capita ratio on the planet.

❄ ❄ ❄ ❄

There is nothing that Finns have been so unanimous about as their sauna. This unanimity has remained unbroken for centuries and is sure to continue as long as there are children born in their native land, as long as the invitation still comes from the porch threshold in the evening twilight: 'The sauna is ready.'

MAILA TALVIO (1871–1951), Finnish writer

❄ ❄ ❄ ❄

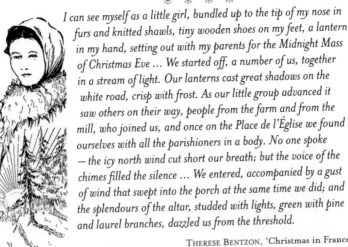

I can see myself as a little girl, bundled up to the tip of my nose in furs and knitted shawls, tiny wooden shoes on my feet, a lantern in my hand, setting out with my parents for the Midnight Mass of Christmas Eve ... We started off, a number of us, together in a stream of light. Our lanterns cast great shadows on the white road, crisp with frost. As our little group advanced it saw others on their way, people from the farm and from the mill, who joined us, and once on the Place de l'Église we found ourselves with all the parishioners in a body. No one spoke — the icy north wind cut short our breath; but the voice of the chimes filled the silence ... We entered, accompanied by a gust of wind that swept into the porch at the same time we did; and the splendours of the altar, studded with lights, green with pine and laurel branches, dazzled us from the threshold.

THERESE BENTZON, 'Christmas in France' published in *The Century Magazine*, describing a Christmas c. 1840

ON CHRISTMAS EVE 1951, HUNDREDS OF FRENCH SCHOOLCHILDREN were part of a large crowd to witness the arresting sight of **Father Christmas being executed** by irate clergymen outside Dijon Cathedral. Against a background of resounding cheers, an eight-foot-high, straw-filled effigy of the jolly man from the North Pole was hanged from the cathedral railings and then set on fire at the beard. Posters were nailed up around the execution site, declaring: 'This is not a boast nor a publicity stunt, but a loud and strong protest against a lie which is incapable of awakening religious sentiment in children.' Dismayed by the growing commercialization and 'paganization' of Christmas, the priests in the diocese of Dijon decided to make public their disappointment with a display of medieval-style brutality. What better symbol of gluttony to bear the brunt of their pious fury than the fat guy in the red suit with all the presents? The pro-Santa lobby in the Dijon district, however, was out in force the following day, forming a rally of their own in the city centre and erecting a number of *Père Noël* effigies in the streets, including a large one on the roof of the City Hall.

❉ ❉ ❉ ❉

IN THE RURAL EAST OF THE NETHERLANDS, YOU MAY STILL HEAR AN eerie sound wafting over the flat fields from the start of Advent through to Epiphany. Some locals there continue to observe the ancient custom of '**blowing the midwinter horn**' to celebrate the coming of Christ. The metre-long horns, carved from elder branches by expert craftsmen, are blown over wells so that the noise will carry for miles around and, the blower hopes, will be answered by another in the distance. The practice is another example of Christians absorbing and reworking pagan traditions to their convenience. In pre-Christian times, the sound of the horn was believed to scare off evil spirits.

❉ ❉ ❉ ❉

Roses are reddish
Violets are bluish
If it weren't for Christmas
We'd all be Jewish.

BENNY HILL, English comedian

BRINGING AN ENTIRE PINE TREE INTO THE HOME AND DECORATING it with candles, gifts and baubles is just one of several Christmas customs that have their origins in Germany. It was from there, too, that the British imported hundreds of ingenious **wooden and mechanical toys** in the nineteenth century as the fashion for Christmas gifts, under the tree and in stockings, began to take hold. The popularity of Christmas trees increased after 1774 when Goethe included the following description in his novel *The Sorrows of Young Werther*:

He began talking of the delight of the children and of that age when the sudden appearance of the Christmas tree, decorated with fruit and sweets, and lighted up with wax candles, caused such transports of joy. 'You too shall have a gift, if you behave well,' said Charlotte, hiding her embarrassment behind a sweet smile.

❋ ❋ ❋ ❋

… But better than the Leipziger Messe, better even than a summer market at Freiburg or at Heidelberg is a Christmas market in any one of the old German cities in the hill country, when the streets and the open places are covered with crisp clean snow, and the mountains are white with it and the moon shines on the ancient houses and the tinkle of sledge bells reaches when you escape from the din of the market … The air is cold and still, and heavy with the scent of the Christmas-trees brought from the forest for the pleasure of the children. Day by day you see the rows of them growing thinner, and if you go to the market on Christmas Eve itself you will find only a few trees left out in the cold. The market is empty, the peasants are harnessing their horses or their oxen, the women are packing up their unsold goods. In every home in the city one of the trees that scented the open air a week ago is shining now with lights and little gilded nuts and apples, and is helping to make that Christmas smell, all compact of the pine forest, wax candles, cakes and painted toys, you must associate so long as you live with Christmas in Germany.

MRS ALFRED SIDGWICK
Home Life in Germany, 1908

GREENLAND, THE WORLD'S LARGEST ISLAND, IS ONE OF THE SEVERAL regions within the Arctic Circle that claim to be the home of Santa Claus. Rivals say the claims of the Danish dependency are undermined by the fact that there is not a single tree, let alone a proper Christmas tree, to be found the length and breadth of a land measuring over half the size of the entire European Union. It is, they say, just lichen, moss and grass – and how on earth do you get presents under that? Greenlanders, of whom there are roughly 50,000, most of them working in the fishing industry, can at least boast two of the world's more unusual Christmas dishes: *mattak* and *kiviak*. *Mattak* is a strip of whaleskin with some blubber inside. It is said to taste a little like coconut, but as it's virtually impossible to chew most people just swallow it. Christmas is the one night of the year when Greenland's men look after the women, and they serve out the *mattak* after coffee which they even stir for the females. *Kiviak* is the raw flesh of the auk, an Arctic bird. It is wrapped in seal skin and buried under heavy stones for several months until it reaches a stage of decomposition from which its taste can only go downhill. *Kiviak*, they say, tastes like very strong Stilton.

❄ ❄ ❄ ❄

THERE ARE OVER 30 MILLION CHRISTIANS LIVING IN THE INDIAN sub-continent, most of them along the coasts of the south and west and in the hill regions of the north-east. The customs of each region differ slightly but in the tropical plains of the south, Christians use **mango and banana trees** as the centrepiece of decorations in the home.

❄ ❄ ❄ ❄

IN 1984, TEMPERATURES IN WASHINGTON WERE IN THE MID-SEVENTIES when President Reagan turned on the lights at the traditional National Christmas Tree ceremony outside the White House.

IT IS AN ANCIENT TRADITION OF IRAQ'S ASSYRIAN CHRISTIAN community to light bonfires of thornbush on Christmas Eve in front of their homes or in their courtyards. If the thorns burn down to ash, it is thought to be good luck for the family in the coming year. Until the 2003 Gulf War, there were one million Christians living **in Iraq**, but, according to the US International Commission on Religious Freedom, as many as half of them are believed to have fled the country as the sectarian violence escalated. As Advent got under way in 2006, the head of Iraq's Christians, Patriarch Emmanuel Delly, appealed to worshippers to refrain from public celebrations at Christmas on security grounds. Many Christians in Iraq were suspected by insurgents of being agents of the Coalition forces.

❄ ❄ ❄ ❄

THE NATIVITY FORMS THE FOCUS of Christmas celebrations in Italy, just as it does in Central and South America and other strongly Catholic cultures. Great effort and creativity goes into the arrangements of manger scenes, but there is little other evidence, in public at least, of Christmas festivities. Tens of thousands of worshippers come to Rome from abroad over the Christmas period – many of them to hear the Pope's Christmas address in St Peter's Square – but they are often surprised by the absence of the gaudy Christmas decorations in shops and streets common in other Western cities and towns. Visitors might also be forgiven for thinking they have flown to Edinburgh by mistake when they hear the unmistakable bleating of the **bagpipes wafting across the piazza**. For centuries, Italian shepherds used to come down from the mountains of Abruzzo and Calabria to Rome and other cities, wearing sheepskin tops and leather breeches, to play their pipes in markets and squares. One other Christmas custom peculiar to the Italians is the belief among children that it is not Father Christmas but a kindly old witch called La Befana who delivers the gifts in the middle of the night. The legend goes that La Befana was following the Three Wise Men to Bethlehem when she got lost and has been wandering the earth ever since.

❄ ❄ ❄ ❄

DIARY ENTRY, 26 December 1770

In the pm myself, Mr Banks [the botanist Joseph], *and all the Gentlemen came on board, and at 6am weigh'd and came to sail with a light breeze at South-West. The* Elgin Indiaman *saluted us with 3 cheers and 13 Guns, and soon after the Garrison with 14, both of which we return'd. Soon after this the Sea breeze set in at North by West, which obliged us to Anchor just without the Ships in the Road. The number of Sick on board at this time amounts to 40 or upwards, and the rest of the Ship's Company are in a weakly condition, having been every one sick except the Sailmaker, an old Man about 70 or 80 years of age; and what is still more extraordinary in this man is his being generally more or less drunk every day. But notwithstanding this general sickness, we lost but 7 men in the whole: the Surgeon, 3 Seamen, Mr. Green's Servant, and Tupia and his Servant, both of which fell a sacrifice to this unwholesome climate before they had reached the object of their wishes. Tupia's death, indeed, cannot be said to be owing wholly to the unwholesome air of Batavia* [Jakarta]; *the long want of a Vegetable Diet, which he had all his life before been used to, had brought upon him all the Disorders attending a Sea life. He was a shrewd, sensible, ingenious man, but proud and obstinate, which often made his situation on board both disagreeable to himself and those about him, and tended much to promote the diseases which put a Period to his Life.*

CAPTAIN COOK

❄ ❄ ❄ ❄

THE NORWEGIAN LANDSCAPE IS CARPETED IN BILLIONS of pine trees, but it wasn't until the early twentieth century that the locals began to follow the German custom of bringing them into the home at Christmas. The traditional feast is eaten on Christmas Eve, after which it is customary for Norwegian families to hold hands and dance around the tree in a ring before opening their presents. Stocking presents are delivered in the night by a dwarf variety of Father Christmas, a bearded troll or gnome called Julenisse.

CHRISTMAS IS BIG IN JAPAN IN SPITE OF THE FACT THAT ONLY I PER cent of the country is Christian. The country has a long history of copying ideas from other cultures and in recent decades Christmas has become a significant event in the Japanese calendar, even though it is not yet an official holiday. Many Japanese don't have the first clue what Christmas is about but they are perfectly happy to decorate their homes, put up Christmas trees, exchange gifts, sing along to 'Ludolph the Lednosed Leindeer' and sit down to a special meal on 25 December. (Following the example of the occupying Americans after the Second World War, many Japanese cook hamburgers or fried chicken.) Tradesmen and big corporations seem to be behind the growing popularity of Christmas, flooding the market with festive goods, and bedecking buildings with Western-style lights and adornments. The experience in Japan illustrates how easily Christmas is absorbed into alien cultures, mainly because it falls at the end of the year when many celebrations are already held. In Japan, you see a lot of drunk people staggering around the streets throughout December, just as you do in Britain, although they are unlikely to be holding a kebab in one hand while trying to fight you with the other. Christmas is *bonenkai* season (literally, 'forget-the-year-party'), when the Japanese eat and drink themselves daft, and wipe the slate on the year that has just passed.

NORWAY HAS A NUMBER OF PECULIAR CHRISTMAS TRADITIONS. THE last Sunday before Christmas in Norway is known as Dirty Sunday because houses are given a thorough cleaning, and anything metal or glass is polished and buffed in preparation for the holiday period. In the western coastal city of Bergen, the children of the surrounding area contribute to the construction of the world's largest gingerbread city. Each year the Norwegian youth pushes back the boundaries of gingerbread creativity and construction to produce ever more original additions to their sprawling confectionary conurbation. In amongst the traditional gingerbread houses and gingerbread men, there are gingerbread boats, gingerbread schools, gingerbread factories and gingerbread dogs and cars.

Did you know that Christmas Day is absolutely the best day to fly? No crowded airports and crowded planes. I always flew to Australia. That's what Christmas was for me — a plane journey to the next tournament.

MONICA SELES, tennis player

✳ ✳ ✳ ✳

CAPTAIN·JOHN·SMITH

CAPTAIN JOHN SMITH, LEADER OF THE FIRST English colony in the United States at Jamestown, spent Christmas 1607 as a captive of the local Algonquian Indians. He later claimed that the chief's beautiful daughter, Pocahontas, saved his life by throwing herself across his body just as he was about to be executed. Otherwise, he seemed to have a very jolly time of it in captivity, writing in his diary:

The extreme winds, rayne, frost and snow caused us to keep Christmas among the savages, where we were never more merry, nor fed on more plenty of good Oysters, Fish, Flesh, Wild Fowl and good bread, nor never had better fires in England.

✳ ✳ ✳ ✳

IN THE CENTRE OF CARACAS, the capital city of **Venezuela**, it is customary for the streets to be blocked off early in the morning during the Christmas period to allow the youth of the city to roller-skate to and from early mass.

✳ ✳ ✳ ✳

FOR CENTURIES THE **JEWISH** communities of Central and Eastern Europe dreaded the Christmas period. Years of being attacked in the streets by drunken Christians taught them to stay in their homes, especially after dark, until the holiday period had passed.

All the Trimmings:

Christmas Odds and Ends

Like all intelligent people, I greatly dislike Christmas. It revolts me to see a whole nation refrain from music for weeks together in order that every man may rifle his neighbour's pockets under cover of a ghastly general pretence of festivity. It really is an atrocious institution this Christmas. We must be gluttonous because it is Christmas. We must be drunken because it is Christmas. We must be insincerely generous; we must buy things that nobody wants, and give them to people we don't like; we must go to absurd entertainments that make even our little children satirical; we must writhe under venal officiousness from legions of freebooters, all because it is Christmas — that is, because the mass of population, including the all-powerful middle-class tradesman, depends on a week of licence and brigandage, waste and intemperance, to clear off its outstanding liabilities at the end of the year.

GEORGE BERNARD SHAW
Music in London

❄ ❄ ❄ ❄

If a man called Christmas Day a mere hypocritical excuse for drunkenness and gluttony, that would be false, but it would have a fact hidden in it somewhere. But when Bernard Shaw says that Christmas Day is only a conspiracy kept up by poulterers and wine merchants from strictly business motives, then he says something which is not so much false as startling and arrestingly foolish. He might as well say that the two sexes were invented by jewellers who wanted to sell wedding rings.

G. K. CHESTERTON
George Bernard Shaw

He [George Bernard Shaw] *writes like a Pakistani who has learned English when he was twelve years old in order to become a chartered accountant.*

JOHN OSBORNE
letter to the *Guardian*

When will artists and printers design us some Christmas cards that will be honest and appropriate to the time we live in? Never was the Day of Peace and Good Will so full of meaning as this year; and never did the little cards, charming as they were, seem so formal, so merely pretty, so devoid of imagination, so inadequate to the festival. This is an age of strange and stirring beauty, of extraordinary romance and adventure, of new joys and pains. And yet our Christmas artists have nothing more to offer us than the old formalism of Yuletide convention. After a considerable amount of searching in the bazaars we have found not one Christmas card that showed even a glimmering of the true romance, which is to see the beauty or wonder or peril that lies around us. Most of the cards hark back to the stage-coach up to its hubs in snow, or the blue bird, with which Maeterlinck penalized us (what has a blue bird got to do with Christmas?), or the open fireplace and jug of mulled claret. Now these things are merry enough in their way, or they were once upon a time; but we plead for an honest romanticism in Christmas cards that will express something of the entrancing color and circumstance that surround us today. Is not a commuter's train, stalled in a drift, far more lively to our hearts than the mythical stage-coach?

Or an inter-urban trolley winging its way through the dusk like a casket of golden light? Or even a country flivver, loaded down with parcels and holly and the Yuletide keg of root beer? Root beer may be but meagre flaggonage compared to mulled claret, but at any rate 'tis honest, 'tis actual, 'tis tangible and potable. And where, among all the Christmas cards, is the airplane, that most marvelous and heart-seizing of all our triumphs? Where is the stately apartment house, looming like Gibraltar against a sunset sky? Must we, even at Christmas time, fool ourselves with a picturesqueness that is gone, seeing nothing of what is round us?

CHRISTOPHER MORLEY, AMERICAN WRITER AND HUMORIST (1890–1957)
Mince Pie, **1918**

THE GIVING OUT OF PRESENTS TO MEMBERS OF the royal household became an important Christmas ritual at Windsor Castle during Queen Victoria's reign. On Christmas Eve, all members were invited to join the Queen and Prince Albert in a ceremony around one of the castle's huge, lavishly decorated trees. Each of the presents piled at the foot of the tree carried nametags with personal messages written by the Queen herself. The gifts were usually small but exquisite, the women receiving jewellery such as lockets and chains, while the men were given accessories such as pearl studs or gold waistcoat buttons. Each member was also given an engraving of the Queen and her family, a practical book such as an almanac and a box of confectionery. After the ceremony, the royal family retired to one of their three sitting rooms to exchange their own gifts in private. Between 1840 and 1857 Victoria gave birth to nine children (who produced a total of 40 children of their own), so the opening of gifts was often a rowdy affair, un-Victorian even. The Windsor House trees were so beautifully decorated that courtiers described them as works of art in their own right. Victoria and Albert had small trees just for themselves placed on tables. In her diary entry for Christmas Day 1850, the young Queen describes her embarrassment at the wealth of presents she received from her husband: *We all assembled and my beloved Albert first took me to my tree and table, covered by such numberless gifts, really too much, too magnificent.* The gifts included an oil painting by John Calcott Horsley, the man who drew the first Christmas card a few years earlier, and a bracelet designed by Albert himself which included a miniature portrait of their daughter Princess Louise.

The Christmas tree

★ Growing Christmas trees is big business. In the United States, there are more than 20,000 Christmas-tree growers and over 12,000 cut-your-own farms. Trees are grown in all 50 states, including Hawaii. In the UK, over seven million trees are grown every year.

★ Each year more and more Christmas trees are being recycled for the benefit of the environment. They are used to make soil erosion barriers and also placed in ponds and lakes for fish shelter.

★ Christmas trees take an average of seven to ten years to mature.

★ It's best not to burn your Christmas tree in the fireplace. The resinous 'green' wood causes creosote to build up, increasing the risk of a chimney fire.

CHRISTMAS CREEP – NOUN. 1) THE COMMERCIAL PHENOMENON WHEREBY retailers push Christmas earlier and earlier in the year in order to lengthen the selling season and steal a march on their rivals. 2) Slightly weird bloke from accounts, who dresses up in hilarious Santa Claus uniform for the office party, makes a drunken pass at the marketing director and, at around midnight, collapses into the buffet table with his face in a bowl of carrot batons.

Britain's favourite carols

'Once in Royal David's City'
'O Come All Ye Faithful'
'Calypso Carol'
'See amid the Winter's Snow'
'O Holy Night'
'It Came upon a Midnight Clear'
'O Little Town of Bethlehem'
'In the Bleak Mid-winter'
'Silent Night'
'Hark the Herald Angels Sing'
    Based on a survey of viewers
    conducted by *Songs of Praise* in
    2005

CHRISTMAS STRESS IS MORE THAN just a hollow expression or an excuse for hard-pressed journalists to fill up the column inches, at least according to a raft of surveys and polls in recent years. The research suggests that most of us do get seriously wound up at Christmas — the very time of year which is supposed to bring us a bit of peace and happiness after a 12-month slog to the end of the calendar. The British Heart Foundation says that 85 per cent of us show significant symptoms of stress while Christmas shopping; 14 per cent of us feel stressed by our neighbours' outdoor light displays, according to research by the Halifax bank (there's a £10 charge for reading that, by the way). Perhaps most depressing and alarming of all, however, is the finding that the stress starts to hit shoppers at around midday on the first Saturday of December. Researchers at Greenwich University say that, by lunchtime on 'Black Saturday', our festive goodwill has been suffocated by the stress of finding Granny a knitted hat. From then on, the boffins claim, the stress mounts and it doesn't go away until the holidays are over. And a Happy New Year to you too.

❄ ❄ ❄ ❄

'CHRISTMAS SHOPPING TURNS FROM A PLEASURE INTO A CHORE THAT raises our heart rates, shuts down body functions like our digestive systems and leaves us physically and mentally exhausted,' says stress expert Neil Shah of the UK's Stress Management Society. 'Research shows that people get particularly stressed when they feel powerless. Shopping is no different.'

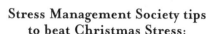
Stress Management Society tips to beat Christmas Stress:

★ Do all your present shopping on one day. Write your list of who you are buying for, then shop via the internet as much as possible to avoid crowds, queues and parking problems.

★ Don't stop for coffee. Caffeine prompts the body to release cortisol, the stress hormone, which will leave you feeling tense. Instead take a bottle of water with you to keep yourself hydrated.

★ Whenever you are in a queue, try this exercise:

breathe in for four counts, hold it for 16 counts, then breathe out for eight counts. This will focus your mind away from your immediate situation and boost the levels of serotonin in your brain.

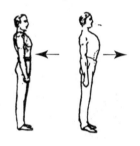

WHEN YOU FINALLY CHUCK THE TURKEY CARCASS ON THE FLOOR FOR your gran and the dog to fight over, get up, reorganize your paper hat and burp your way into the sitting room to watch the *Vicar of Dibley Xmas Cracker*, pause a moment to reflect on the damage you and your family have just inflicted on the environment. Of the eight million Christmas trees we buy each year, three-quarters are burnt or dumped in landfill. (A round of applause for the two million people who go to the small-to-medium effort of taking their trees to a recycling depot.) More than a billion Christmas cards and 83 square kilometres of wrapping paper, an area the size of Paris, will suffer the same fate; over 3,000 tons of kitchen foil for the turkey, the equivalent of 20 jumbo jets, will end up being buried in the ground and almost 50 per cent of the toys you give your children will be thrown out by Easter. In 2006, the Liberal Democrat Environment spokesman Chris Huhne pointed out that the 125,000 tons of plastic packaging we throw out at Christmas is the equivalent of more than a million John Prescotts. And if that doesn't scare you into recycling ...

FOR DECADES PEOPLE HAVE BEEN SPENDING BEYOND THEIR BUDGETS at Christmas but in recent years debt levels in Britain have soared, causing significant problems for thousands of individuals and households. In January 2007, 1.2 million bills went unpaid as spending sprees and early December payments hit people's pockets in the New Year. Credit cards and council tax are the bills that the hard-up are most likely to skip paying, followed by mobile phones and utilities. The Citizens Advice Bureau saw an increase of 15 per cent in people coming to discuss debt problems compared to January 2006. A quarter of all those who walked into their bureaux in the financial year 2005/2006 had got themselves into debt difficulties.

Some tips from the Citizens Advice Bureau

* Avoid borrowing further to try to pay off existing debt.

* Talk to your creditors. They will sometimes be more understanding than you expect.

* Work out how much you owe and then prioritize your payments.

* Only offer to pay off debts at a rate that suits you. Don't get panicked into offering more than you can afford.

* Don't pay for debt advice. Citizens Advice, independent experts in dealing with creditors, will help you for free.

* Set up a standing order to save a little each month, and slowly build up a fund for Christmas or holidays.

WHAT'S WRONG WITH WALES IN DECEMBER? SEVEN PER CENT OF Welsh people spend their Christmas abroad, twice as many per capita as the English and the Scots.

※ ※ ※ ※

YORKSHIRE FOLK LEAVE THEIR CHRISTMAS SHOPPING LATER THAN anyone else in Britain. Over a third of people living in 'God's Own County' wait until Christmas Eve before hitting the shops. Yorkshire people are also among the lowest Christmas spenders of all of the regions in the UK.

CHRISTMAS IS BY FAR THE BUSIEST AND MOST IMPORTANT TRADING period of the year for UK retailers. Between 40 and 60 per cent of the turnover of larger outlets is generated between November and January – a period that has been awkwardly dubbed 'the Golden Triangle' by some business school whizz-kid with a shoddy understanding of the dimensions of time and space. For most of us, Christmas is a pleasant, traditional family knees-up. Spare a thought then for the analysts amongst us for whom Christmas is just one long space–time retail continuum.

Christmas tree tips

by Christmas Day because they dry out quickly in centrally heated homes, or if they are placed in rooms with open fires. Your tree will last longer if you stand it up in a bucket of stones and water it every few days or so.

★ It's hard to tell the age of a Christmas tree by looking at it, so shake it to see if the needles fall off, or run your fingers along a branch against the flow.

★ Weight is another telltale sign. Fresh trees are much heavier than older ones because they're still full of sap.

★ If you plant out a root-balled or container tree after Christmas, bear in mind that most pine trees are vigorous growers that reach great heights.

★ Many trees look as if they were grown in Chernobyl

★ When discarding your tree, avoid carpeting your house in millions of unhooverable needles by wrapping it in a sheet before carrying it outside.

★ Bushy trees with lots of dense branches look better wrapped in tinsel, while the more sparsely branched varieties suit just a few wisps of tinsel and lots of hanging decorations. Don't ask why.

IT'S BEST TO PICK HOLLY A FEW WEEKS BEFORE YOU intend to use it as a decoration and then store it because if you leave it much later than early December the birds will have snaffled all the berries. To keep it fresh, treat holly like cut flowers and place the stems in a vase of water, or stick them into a bucket of moist sand. Holly will stay fresher for longer if, as with your tree, you keep the stems away from dehydrating heat sources like radiators and out of direct sunlight.

❄ ❄ ❄ ❄ ❄

Gentlemen do not care for the pretty trifles and decorations that delight ladies; and as for real necessities, they are apt to go and buy anything that is a convenience just as soon as it is discovered. Knick-knacks, articles of china, etc., are generally useless to them. A Lady cannot give a gentleman a gift of great value because he would certainly feel bound to return one still more valuable and thus her gift would lose all its grace and retain only a selfish commercial aspect.

What, then, shall she give? Here is the woman's advantage. She has her hands, while men must transact all their present giving in hard cash. She can hem fine handkerchiefs — and in order to give them intrinsic value, if their relationship warrants such a favour, she can embroider the name or monogram with her own hair. If the hair is dark it has a very pretty, graceful effect, and the design may be shaded by mingling the different hair of the family. We knew a gentleman who for years lost every handkerchief he took to the office; at length his wife marked them with her own hair, and he never lost another. Such gifts are made precious by love, time and talent.

The bare fact of rarity can raise an object commercially valueless, to an aesthetic level. Souvenirs from famous places or of famous people, a bouquet of wild thyme from Mount Hymettus, an ancient Jewish shekel or Roman coin, etc. All such things are very suitable as presents to gentlemen and will be far more valued than pins, studs, etc., which only represent a certain number of dollars and cents. Do not give a person who is socially your equal a richer present than he is able to give you. He will be more mortified than pleased. But between equals it is often an elegance to disregard cost and depend on rarity, because gold cannot always purchase it. Still between very rich people presents should also be very rich or else their riches are set above their friendship and generosity.

Harpers Bazaar, 1879

MARTHA STEWART'S
CHRISTMAS HOLIDAY TO-DO LIST

1 December: *Blanch carcass from Thanksgiving turkey. Spray-paint gold, turn upside down and use as a sleigh to hold Christmas cards.*

2 December: *Contact local choir to record outgoing Christmas message for answering machine.*

3 December: *Repaint Sistine Chapel ceiling with mocha trim.*

4 December: *Get new eyeglasses. Grind lenses self.*

5 December: *Fax family Christmas newsletter to Pulitzer committee for consideration.*

6 December: *Debug Windows '95.*

9 December: *Align carpets to adjust for curvature of Earth.*

11 December: *Lay Fabergé egg.*

12 December: *Take dog apart. Disinfect. Reassemble.*

13 December: *Collect dentures. They make excellent pastry cutters, particularly for decorative piecrusts.*

14 December: *Install plumbing in gingerbread house.*

15 December: *Adjust legs of chairs so all Christmas dinner guests will be the same height when sitting down.*

16 December: *Dip sheep and cows in egg whites and roll in icing sugar to add a festive sparkle to the pasture.*

17 December: *Drain city reservoir; refill with mulled cider, orange slices and cinnamon sticks.*

18 December: *Float votive candles in toilet tank.*

20 December: *Seed clouds for white Christmas.*

21 December: *Do festive good deed. Go to several stores. Be seen engaged in last-minute Christmas shopping, thus making many people feel less inadequate than they really are.*

23 December: *Organize spice racks by genus and phylum.*

24 December: *Build snowman in exact likeness of God.*

25 December: *Bear son. Swaddle. Lay in colour-coordinated manger scented with homemade potpourri.*

New Year's Eve: *Give staff their resolutions. Call a friend in each time zone of the world as the clock strikes midnight in that country.*

ANON

IN 1975, AMERICAN SELF-IMPROVEMENT GURU AND LIFE COACH WERNER Erhard set a world record of handwriting 62,824 Christmas cards from his home in San Francisco. He was very disappointed to receive only three in return. (Just kidding, Werner, I'm sure you got loads.)

✳ ✳ ✳ ✳

Once again, we come to the Holiday Season, a deeply religious time that each of us observes, in his own way, by going to the mall of his choice.

ANON

✳ ✳ ✳ ✳

I stopped believing in Santa Claus when I was six. Mother took me to see him in a department store and he asked for my autograph.

SHIRLEY TEMPLE (1928–), American actress and diplomat

✳ ✳ ✳ ✳

As Christmas decorations are 'but for a season' it is not necessary that they should be of expensive materials, or elaborate workmanship; on the contrary, the cheapness and simplicity of the means used in producing the effect, seem often to enhance the pleasure received from looking upon it.

Cassell's Book of the Household,
1878

✳ ✳ ✳ ✳

I love Christmas. I receive a lot of wonderful presents I can't wait to exchange.

HENRY YOUNGMAN (1906–98),
British-American comedian

198

For common gifts, necessity makes pertinences and beauty every day, and one is glad when an imperative leaves him no option, since if the man at the door have no shoes, you have not to consider whether you could procure him a paint-box. And as it is always pleasing to see a man eat bread, or drink water, in the house or out of doors, so it is always a great satisfaction to supply these first wants. Necessity does everything well … Next to things of necessity, the rule for a gift, which one of my friends prescribed, is, that we might convey to some person that which properly belonged to his character, and was easily associated with him in thought. But our tokens of compliment and love are for the most part barbarous. Rings and other jewels are not gifts, but apologies for gifts. The only gift is a portion of thyself. Thou must bleed for me. Therefore the poet brings his poem; the shepherd, his lamb; the farmer, corn; the miner, a gem; the sailor, coral and shells; the painter, his picture; the girl, a handkerchief of her own sewing. This is right and pleasing, for it restores society in so far to its primary basis, when a man's biography is conveyed in his gift, and every man's wealth is an index of his merit. But it is a cold, lifeless business when you go to the shops to buy me something, which does not represent your life and talent, but a goldsmith's. This is fit for kings, and rich men who represent kings, and a false state of property, to make presents of gold and silver stuffs, as a kind of symbolical sin-offering, or payment of black-mail …

He is a good man who can receive a gift well. We are either glad or sorry at a gift, and both emotions are unbecoming. Some violence, I think, is done, some degradation borne, when I rejoice or grieve at a gift. I am sorry when my independence is invaded or when a gift comes from such as do not know my spirit, and so the act is not supported; and if the gift pleases me overmuch, then I should be ashamed that the donor should read my heart, and see that I love his commodity and not him. The gift, to be true, must be the flowing of the giver unto me, correspondent to my flowing unto him. When the waters are at level, then my goods pass to him, and his to me. All his are mine, all mine his. I say to him, How can you give me this pot of oil, or this flagon of wine, when all your oil and wine is mine, which belief of mine this gift seems to deny? Hence the fitness of beautiful, not useful things for gifts.

RALPH WALDO EMERSON (1803–82)
Essays and English Traits, 1844

❋　❋　❋　❋

MISTLETOE, A PARASITIC EVERGREEN SHRUB GROWING HIGH IN THE branches of old trees, is becoming increasingly difficult to find in Britain. The most common host is the apple tree and it is no coincidence that mistletoe has been disappearing at the same alarming rate that our orchards have been shrinking in size and number over the past 50 years. Most of the mistletoe we buy in the shops comes from Normandy, where the apple industry continues to thrive.

An ornament in which children delight, the idea of which comes from Germany, is a jolly little black chimney sweep, with his funny broom held high in the air. He wears a peaked white hat and carries a bag filled with goodies. He is made entirely of prunes — one for the head, two for the body, one for each arm, one for each hand, two for each leg, and one for each foot. The prunes are strung together with a coarse needle and thread. If, when made, he is too limber, give him a backbone by running a slender stick through the back of his head and body. Give him a paper hat shaped like a wide-mouthed horn, and make a paper face; then tie the sheer white bag across his shoulders, fasten it at the side with a pin and fill the bag with sweets; the broom can be fashioned of a wooden toothpick with a bunch of broom straws bound on one end. The happy child who receives him from the tree may devour the prunes when tired of the toy.

The Delineator Magazine, December 1901

❄   ❄   ❄   ❄

What funny things to give a baby — gold and myrrh and frankincense. That's men all over! It wouldn't cross their minds to bring a shawl!

MOIRA ANDREW, POET AND AUTHOR

❄   ❄   ❄   ❄

Christmas started going wrong for me when I was about 14. All I wanted was some clothes, some money, some make-up, some jewellery, some perfume, some platforms, some tights, some electric curlers, a handbag, a leather jacket, a Jackie *annual, a selection box, a* Pick of the Pops *album featuring a girl on the cover wearing kinky boots full of really bad cover versions, a stereo, a telly for my room and my own front door key. What I actually got was an anglepoise lamp so that I didn't strain my eyes whilst I did my homework. My mother ended up with that anglepoise lamp — she wore it all Christmas Day, tightly wrapped around her neck.*

JENNY ECLAIR (1960–), English Comedian
The Book of Bad Behaviour

Acknowledgements

The author and publishers are grateful for permission to reproduce extracts from the following:

The Diaries of Bernard Shaw, *Our Theatres in the Nineties* and *Music in London* by Bernard Shaw, reprinted by permission of The Society of Authors, on behalf of the Bernard Shaw Estate.

The Book of Bad Behaviour by Jenny Eclair, copyright © Jenny Eclair, 2004, Virgin Books Ltd.

A Child's Christmas in Wales by Dylan Thomas, copyright © 1954 by New Directions Publishing Corp. Reprinted by permission of New Directions Publishing Corp. and David Higham Associates.

The Diaries of Evelyn Waugh by Michael Davie (ed.), published by Weidenfeld and Nicolson. Reprinted by permission of The Orion Publishing Group.

Food and Feast in Medieval England by P. W. Hammond, copyright © Sutton Publishing.

A Better Class of Person and a letter to the *Guardian* by John Osborne, reprinted by permission of The Arvon Foundation.

Cider with Rosie by Laurie Lee, published by Chatto & Windus. Reprinted by permission of The Random House Group Ltd and PFD on behalf of The Estate of Laurie Lee © Laurie Lee, 1959.

Index

BB 1/08